FOR PRAYING OUT LOUD

Interfaith Prayers for Public Occasions

L. ANNIE FOERSTER

SKINNER HOUSE BOOKS
BOSTON

Thanks to Meg Riley, UUA Director of Advocacy and Witness,
for her help in collecting public prayers of peace, dedication, advocacy, and justice.

Published by Skinner House Books.
Skinner House Books is an imprint of the
Unitarian Universalist Association,
a liberal religious organization with more
than 1,000 congregations in the U.S. and Canada.
25 Beacon Street, Boston, MA 02108-2800.

Text design by Kathryn Sky-Peck.
Cover design by Kimberly Glyder.
Printed in Canada.

ISBN 1-55896-450-9

06 05 04 03
10 9 8 7 6 5 4 3 2 1

Library of Congress Cataloging-in-Publication Data

Foerster, L. Annie.
    For praying out loud : interfaith prayers for public occasions / L. Annie Foerster.
        p. cm.
    Includes index.
    ISBN 1-55896-450-9 (alk. paper)
        1. Unitarian Universalist Association—Prayer books and devotions—English.
    2. Pastoral prayers. I. Title.
    BX9855.F64 2003
    291.3'8--dc21   2002042564

Note to our readers: Do you have any original public prayers that you would like
considered for publication? Please send them with your contact information to
Editor, Skinner House Books, 25 Beacon Street, Boston, MA 02108,
skinner_submissions@uua.org.

CONTENTS

INTRODUCTION

SOME FORM OF PRAYER is part of every religious community. The act of praying or meditating is so universal, in fact, that one wonders if the need to reach out beyond ourselves in thought and word is simply part of the human condition. In many faith traditions, prayers are ritualized and specific. A body of common prayer literature provides familiarity and comfort, as well as connection within the faith community. Community prayers, such as those used in worship, gather the participants into a common mental and spiritual space, upholding the tenets of the faith and offering support and inspiration to the faithful.

Public prayers, in contrast, are often shared among partic-ipants of diverse faiths. Interfaith celebrations and secular gatherings require a spiritual language that will, on the one hand, invoke a sense of the holy, and on the other, provide a common ground of belonging for all present. At such public events, however, common prayers may fail to connect people across denominational and interfaith divides. We need a new literature for praying out loud.

Sixteenth-century clergyman Francis David said, "In this world there have always been many opinions about faith and salvation. You need not think alike to love alike." We need to listen to one another. When Buddhist and Muslim temples are built alongside synagogues and churches, when "holy wars" are fought all over the world, then mutual respect and inclusion are essential in our dealings with one another. Where better to address our differences as well as our common beliefs than in prayer at public events?

This can be challenging for clergy and lay people alike. Those from backgrounds in which prayers are prescribed by format and language, those who believe that *ecumenical* and *interfaith* mean the same thing, often have trouble reaching out to others of different faiths.

I once participated in a Martin Luther King Day event, in which a Jewish woman, a Hindu man, an Islamic teenager, and a Buddhist priest each offered his or her respective faith's blessings to the congregation. But they squirmed in discomfort when a Christian minister offered a prayer from his own tradition that included the words, "Jesus is the *only* way to salvation and reconciliation with God." Naturally, this offended the non-Christian guests, and an opportunity for public healing was missed.

If we are to be successful, we must learn to include even followers of faiths we know little about. We need to become passionately inclusive, beginning with our universal concerns for other living things: children, trees, pets.

The goal of this book of collected prayers is to help us evoke all of creation as our palette for public worship. When nothing and no one is left out of our prayers—when everything in creation is present—it is easy to reach the heart of God *and* of the gathered community. When we understand and believe that the holy is at the center of our gathered community, our prayers will have more impact, both spiritually and secularly.

As a Unitarian Universalist parish minister, I belong to a faith tradition that is frequently mined for inclusive prayers because it is non-creedal. *For Praying Out Loud* is a result of my years as the designated prayer leader at interfaith events. This book includes my own prayers as well as those of colleagues, both Unitarian Universalist and others.

The first part of the book focuses on the challenge of writing inclusive public prayers. The second part is a collection of successful inclusive prayers, which can be delivered as written, adapted to better fit your own occasions, or used as inspiration to create your own.

Here is my first prayer for you: May you feel comfort and joy in letting go of formal structure and rules when praying in public. May you reach out equally to all within the sound of your voice and the embrace of your heart. May you inspire others with your prayerful poetry and prose.

HOW TO WELCOME THE WHOLE
COMMUNITY THROUGH PRAYER

THE PROBLEM WITH TRADITION is that it gets to be a habit. Habits can dull creativity if we let them. But creativity is necessary for change. If we are to be inclusive in the way we pray in public, we need create some new traditions.

Traditional prayers were once new. The Psalms in the Hebrew bible were created by poets and lovers. We need to learn to think like poets and lovers about the things for which we pray.

Many traditional prayers were created for the solitary worshiper. They were designed to keep one focused, especially on the lessons of the Holy. Although public prayer requires a different focus, we do not need to begin with a completely blank page. If we look carefully at traditional prayers, both their limitations and their possibilities become apparent.

Many of the traditional prayers can be used in diverse settings as long as we make sure they are inclusive. For example, to end his prayer dedicating a new hospital wing ("Written on the Heart"), Rabbi Gary P. Zola said, "We are grateful for the strength we find in the company of those dedicated to healing the body and the mind, to acts of loving-kindness, and to the betterment of the human condition. In this spirit of dedication, I rely on the words of the Psalmist of old in expressing our deeply felt sentiments of thanksgiving: 'Let the favor of the Eternal One be upon us; let all that we put our hands to prosper. O prosper the work of our hands!' " *(Psalm 91:17)*

For a service focusing on prejudice against the elderly ("The Issues That Divide Us"), I wanted a prayer that would reframe my listeners' viewpoints and ask them to support one another in breaking down the barriers of prejudice. I wanted a prayer that asked listeners to be more welcoming of diversity. I didn't ask that God change them; but that they change themselves. I chose to include other prejudices beside age-ism in order to make a stronger case: "May we look with the eyes of spirit and the eyes of heart to see beyond the barriers we built to cloak our fears, and the monuments we erected to celebrate our foolishness. These are our prayers of diversity."

One of the most famous of all traditional prayers is the Christian blessing known as the Beatitudes. I have heard many variations on this prayer, but none so successful as "Blessed Are the Just" by Rev. Richard Gilbert. The occasion was the inauguration of the New York attorney general at City Hall in Rochester. Gilbert did not follow tradition by asking God to make this public servant a better politician. Instead, he used the Confucian model by simply stating, in the form of the Beatitudes, what defines a good statesman: "Blessed are the just, for they have their reward in indestructible integrity; … Blessed are they who serve the public good, for their reward is in being used."

At an interfaith Thanksgiving Eve service near Seattle, Washington, participants brought canned goods to donate to the Food Bank, and the offering went to the same agency. The service was adequately attended; people were happy to join together to help a favorite local charity. Still, the annual coming together felt more like an exercise in tolerance than one of acceptance. Watching the participants, one could almost guess each person's denominational affiliation by watching his or her attentiveness, or lack of it, during specific prayers. It was okay to have different parts of the service reflect different traditions, but the fervent adherence to each tradition seemed to stress differences instead of similarities. A prayer ("Aren't We All One Family?") that called attention to our common membership in the human family, rather than our individual membership in a particular church, would have served the purpose more effectively: "Let our prayer be heard, for aren't we all one family, with the same wants and needs?"

It is not necessary or advisable to reduce our individual traditions and writings to a bland pap in order to make them more inclusive. Some traditions are universal, and we can adapt others to be so without diminishing them.

Rev. Jill Job Saxby found an inspirational connection between the construction of a new bridge in her community and a question in Isaiah 40:12, "Who has measured the waters in the hollow of his hand and marked off the heavens with a span ...?" The bridge opened with a day-long celebration, and at the invocation Saxby built her imagery around this passage. Her prayer, "To Build a Bridge," has three distinct parts. In the first, she addresses the holy by many names and offers thanks—thanks for "the abundant gifts of the earth and the sea," for "sustenance and creativity," for "the day," for "those who made the celebration possible," and for "the gift of community."

In the second part of her prayer, Saxby speaks poetically of a bridge between past and present, present and future. "We are connected also to the generations to come, who will cross over and sail under this bridge long after we are gone."

Finally, she makes an analogy to the bridges that connect individuals and communities of diversity. "We also pray for the vision and the perseverance necessary to build new bridges of opportunity, justice and equality within our communities." Throughout she is faithful to the original imagery—measuring the waters (and our differences) and marking them off with a span (bridging not only land masses, but temporal masses, political masses, and the mass of humanity). Saxby's imagery would fit many different occasions in which people need to "get over" their differences.

CREATING A HOLY SPACE

THOSE WHO PLAN SECULAR PROGRAMS that include public
prayer—rallies, commemorations, graduations, ground-
breaking ceremonies, or political events—often include the
religious portion of the program as an after-thought: "Maybe
we ought to have a prayer in here somewhere. Any of you
know a minister we might call?" I find that the invitation to
pray is seldom an explicit request to evoke the Holy. Perhaps
that's implicit in the request, "Maybe you can set a tone for
our meeting, Reverend." Yet, sometimes when I enter a noisy
hall before a meeting is to start, I have the feeling that the real
reason I'm there is to get the participants quieted down and
ready for work.

Without specific direction, those of us who create and
lead public prayers must try to create a sacred space, where

people will feel inspirited and inspired. Rev. Margaret Keip is very good at this. Reading her "Prayer for Peace," one can almost hear the dramatic pauses she must have taken as she spoke the first three lines: "There are one hundred and fifty of us here today. One hundred and fifty uniquely personal faiths. One hundred and fifty different understandings of God." Then she compared her audience to the cosmos: "In this way we are not unlike this world."

When she had drawn a picture with her words—"Us" in the center of "All" as the Holy Space—she invited everyone to pray with her, silently in his or her own way. Then she brought the sacred circle to completion, with the inspired suggestion that we "become verbs."

In a "Prayer of Presence," at another event, Keip created a "holy space" of community by inviting people to be present to one another: "Make this community of being, which we together are, now—tangible. Feel it. It is real. We are real. We are here. We are now. We can never be anywhere else." But before she spoke these powerful words, she invited the participants to touch one another: "clasp a hand, touch a shoulder, link an arm." She asked for community and prayerful space. Before her final blessing, she described what would happen if the participants *denied* community, "withheld from this moment." Essentially, her prayer says, there are consequences for denying community.

Inviting participation is a large part of creating a prayerful space. The power of touch, a call to name what is happening, and the request for involvement are compelling spiritual prompts to most gatherings. Responsive readings, litanies, and call-and-response singing are other familiar ways of involving people.

In a memorial service for Rev. Martin Luther King, Rev. George A. Robinson III uses the questions "Who?" and "Why?" as a litany ("Keepers of the Dream"), repeating them over and over again, letting the community answer. "Who," he prayed, "are keepers of the dream?" In responding, I believe each person found him- or herself included in the holy space.

Even when the planners of an event are clergy, it is sometimes difficult to create an inclusive service out of their various faith traditions. It is difficult, but not impossible.

In 1998, the Jewish community of Cincinnati, Ohio, donated a peace garden to the city, located in the city zoo. Rabbi Gary P. Zola, who planned the dedication ceremony, believed that since the gift was for the *whole* city, the dedication needed to have larger religious participation. He invited me, a female Unitarian Universalist minister, as well as a black Baptist minister, to speak at the ceremony. But instead of each of us offering a prayer, which he reasoned would "sound like every other gathering where each clergy prays to his own group," Rabbi

Zola suggested we each read a poem of our choosing that spoke to our religious philosophy.

Two weeks before the dedication, however, none of us had found a poem that suited the occasion. We met and began to talk about what each of us held to be the essence of peace. Our strongest point of agreement was that peace was more than the absence of war. I volunteered to write a poem on the theme, which all of us could read responsively. The poem, "Let Us Learn Peace," turned out to be very much like a prayer, although its tone was probably quite different from the prayers that each of us separately would have offered. Each of its four verses suggests that peace is more than the absence of something: of worry, discordance, tension, and war. Each verse ends with an invitation to seek something—contentment, harmony, serenity, and amity—in order to "learn peace."

When creating sacred space, the opening words of a traditional worship service—either public or semi-public—are a good way to invoke the Holy. Sometimes just reminding people why they are present and what is expected of them as participants is enough to set the tone. When many religious traditions are included in a service or program, the participants are often grateful for any clues and cues they are given. Even members of the predominant tradition at an event are not always aware of what is expected of them in every circumstance. The installation of a colleague some years ago was an opportunity to educate others in creating prayerful space: "This is no ordinary thing we are called to do this evening," I explained in "This Sacred Moment." "And we are no ordinary people who do it. If you invest in this moment, you can lend it the spirit of your hopes and dreams, grant it the soul of your vision and desire, give it the empowerment of your wisdom and love."

WRITING THE PRAYERS

THE CREATIVE PROCESS IS DIFFICULT to explain, and often varies, from person to person and even for the same person at different times. Sometimes it helps to look for a prevailing metaphor and develop it. Sometimes it's easier to imagine what you are working on as poetry instead of prayer. Sometimes it's simply a matter of figuring out what needs to be said and finding a new or unusual way to say it. Creativity tends to be right-brain–oriented, with feelings rather than intellect at the forefront.

The same devices that enable us to remember and be touched by poetry lend themselves to the inspirational effects and ultimate recollection of prayers. They include:

Metaphors and *similes* keep a mental image before us that connects us to past or present, to one another, or to the occasion of the prayer. A simile uses direct comparison: "This gathering is like the world." A metaphor assumes the comparison, as Jill Job Saxby did when she called those assembled at the dedication of a bridge "bridge-builders."

Alliteration and *rhythm* use the repetition of sound or beat to emphasize and drive home a point. Alliteration is the repetition of initial consonants: "hearts of hallowed hope"; "minds of measured meaning." The use of rhythm can include the repetition of a phrase—"Blessed are they who ..."—or of a particular accented beat.

Hyperbole and *synecdoche* use strong contrast, exaggeration, and diminution. Hyperbole is usually an exaggeration for effect: "We have waited for an eternity." The use of synecdoche, substituting a part for the whole or the whole for a part, is common in everyday speech, as when we speak of ten "head" of cattle, meaning the entire animal.

Rhyming, puns, and allusions are other tools traditionally used in poetry that can add to a prayer's effect. Before you begin to write your prayer, read some of your favorite poetry for inspiration.

Rev. Kathleen McTigue uses the metaphor of weaving and the loom in her prayer ("We Are Woven Together") for an Interfaith Alliance chapter meeting: "We seek a union woven through choice and intent, through time and attention, through respect and compassion, until we recognize that we have become a whole cloth ..." But McTigue doesn't stop there; she harvests the richness of her metaphor when, later in her prayer, she adds, "Each of us can hear, in the beating of our own hearts, the ancient rhythm of the loom at work. We are woven together."

Rev. Katie Stein Sather and Rev. Susan Suchocki Brown both use rhythm and repetition in their prayers, but in very different ways. Rev. Sather found a poetic formula for saying grace in which she repeated a litany (and a variation on it) for every blessing. That the grace was spoken at a 4-H dinner allowed her to focus her blessing on head, heart, hands, and health, beginning each of the four sections with "Let us give thanks" (or "Let us be grateful") and ending it with the echo-statement, "We give thanks" ("We are grateful"). The result, "Let Us Be Grateful," is a brief but memorable prayer of gratitude.

Brown began her prayer ("Together in Love") for the opening of a Martin Luther King, Jr. celebration in much the same way, but built up to the heart of it by adding phrases, one by one, and then repeating the whole larger phrase. "Let us be," she said. Then, "Let us be together,"—changing the meaning ever so slightly. Then, "Let us be together in love," she prayed, continuing to add other ways that listeners could experience togetherness.

Some readings are outwardly more poem than prayer—there is no address of the Holy, nor any whisper of "amen" to close it. There are no petitions, no gratitude, no mention of the gathered community. But "Creation in Three-Quarter Time with Mixed Metaphor," offers a metaphoric song as a new creation myth, to be heard as prayer—"There was space, but no beginning, and in the space were spaces, and between the spaces, stars"—implying, or at least intending to imply, both hope and gratitude. I also used outrageous metaphors for a sense of levity: "And their Intimacy made Possibility and Potential—Hmmm, and Maybe, and Yes! A kind of blind date between old friends; a kind of dream without sleeping." The prayer has worked (that is, affected people) on many different types of occasions. People laugh, nod, comment and discuss it afterward. It is another encouragement to let go of traditional assumptions of what a prayer is, or should be.

For the invocation at a Martin Luther King, Jr. breakfast meeting, Rev. Victor Carpenter chose to tell the story of Rosa Parks, the march on Selma, and the death of King as his prayer. He used a "biblical" voice to tell this modern story, beginning: "And it came to pass in those days that the spirit of God visited a young woman whose name was Rosa."

Story-telling is very effective in getting people's attention, especially if you use a familiar format for telling it. Throughout his prayer, "Prophet in the Wilderness of Racism," Carpenter maintained the role of story-teller, ending it with a prediction:

"And so it is given to us in these latter days that by our efforts (as God shall help us), the oppressed shall receive justice, the righteous shall receive their reward, and peace shall flow down like a mighty stream."

The Jewish tradition also lends itself to story-telling. For instance, at another Martin Luther King Day celebration in Cincinnati, Rabbi Gary P. Zola told the story of a hiker who found a pure spring and decided to trace it to its source. The font, he discovered, was a tiny hole in the mountain forest floor, yet the water that spilled forth could not be stopped and was so powerful that it spread its life-giving force throughout the valley. Proceeding directly from the story into prayer ("A Tiny Wellspring, A Thundering River"), without benefit of address, Rabbi Zola said, "The man we honor this day was a wellspring. His ideals, his convictions, his faith bubbled up from their sacred source within and pushed their way up through the mossy overgrowth of bigotry and intolerance, bursting forth into the light of a better day."

The most important consideration in creating an inclusive, effective public prayer is to recognize the path of least resistance—whether it is tradition, habit, laziness, or lack of time—and override it. I learned this as a seminary student, when I was asked to write the closing prayer for my gradua-tion ceremony. I was given no topic, no maximum length, no liturgy or program, and no hint of what the other speakers might be saying. Still captive in my role as a student, I thought of this prayer as my final test, my last grade.

As part of the process of becoming a minister, I had been learning to let go of the foolish human belief that I was in control of my life, or needed to be. I knew I didn't want to say the usual things, such as "Bless these students as they go forward," or, "Help us to remember to be humble." Once I admitted to myself that I didn't know what to say—didn't even know what I *wanted* to say—the prayer almost wrote itself. I realized that everyone at that service could probably say the same thing: "I don't know what I want, but that doesn't end the wanting or asking. I don't even know what I need, but that doesn't lessen my determination to go looking for it." It is the human condition. I decided to put my own sense of inadequacy in the spotlight of the prayer. I called it: "Prayer of Petition (When You Don't Know What You Want or Need)." It was the first time I'd ever given a title to one of my prayers.

Seven years later, after serving two small, yoked churches, watching them reach, stumble, and grow, I was even more aware that we often don't know what we need, even when we think we know what we want. When I was asked to give the opening prayer on Charter Sunday for a brand-new church in Tualitin, Oregon, this thought was on my mind. I knew of the new congregation's excitement, and the nothing-can-stop-us-now attitude of its leaders. I also knew from experience that such start-ups are not without peril. I chose to offer three blessings to the group ("Why Bouquets Have Nettles")— blessings that would honor their optimism for the future, while grounding them in the realities of the present: "May the far-sighted vision they have of possibilities inherent in this great venture, be dimmed to expedient myopia, so they may not be frightened by the arduousness of the path just ahead."

Of course, one doesn't have to be clergy to pray. Lay people often don't have the bias of religious education to block their attempts at inclusivity. Shortly before his death, Jim Berry wrote a prayer ("A Home for Rest, Peace, and Love") for the dedication of his church's memorial garden, asking the spirit of the Holy to "take care for this place." He listed the attributes of those who are memorialized there, including "those whose quest had not yet found answer," and asked that they "find in this place rest, peace, and love."

A local anti-bias task force asked Rev. Beth Graham to offer the closing prayer at its First Harmony Concert, at which it also announced the winner of a student essay contest on "How Racism Has Affected Me." For her theme, Beth chose "We have gathered as one," listing in her prayer ("Knitted Together By Music") the many ways in which the gathered community was kindred and how it was varied. "Knitted together by so many strands of music, from so many different religious and ethnic communities ..." Her litany noted the factors that had brought them together and the dreams they shared for their future. The result was a warm embrace of all participants and all efforts, a blessing of intimacy and harmony. Graham used the tools of poetry-writing to draw her listeners into the sacred circle. The rhythm of her prayer—repetitive and soothing, building to a crescendo of hope—like the rhythm of the songs that preceded it, offers a compelling encouragement to listen and take part.

A prayer I wrote for the opening of an annual Gay Pride Interfaith Service is also appropriate for other situations in which diverse people gather. Each year that I participate in this service, I struggle with the complexity of the issues and emotions surrounding it. On the one hand are the participants and their supporters—proud, angry, hurt, afraid, compassionate, and hopeful; and on the other, its detractors—also angry and afraid—who tend to denigrate this gathering community as "just another bunch of queers." I wanted to celebrate that while we come together for a common purpose, we are richly diverse. The title, "Let Me Tell You Who We Are," was a response to a letter to the editor in a local newspaper complaining about the "degenerates and perverts" who were that day's participants.

"Let me tell you who we are," I wanted to say to the letter's writer. "We are as diverse as the gods we honor—and as rich." Instead, I addressed my words to the participants themselves and to the diverse forms of the God they worshipped: "Spirit of Ages, Creator of Life and Love, whose names and attributes are infinite, knowable and unknown; oh, Spirit, hear our prayers. Our names, too, are many. Let me tell you who we are." The most important idea for me was in a line in the last paragraph, which read, "It is important to know us in our rich diversity, for we struggle to know ourselves, and one another."

Isn't this the key to living in harmony with diversity? Isn't this what we come up against in relation to our politics, our faith, the color of our skin and our reaching out to one another for love and understanding—this struggle to know ourselves, and one another? At the center of the gathered community dwells the Holy. Sometimes, when people gather, they *are* the prayer. Their presence, their relationships, their interaction, their longing for one another, speak *to* the Holy and *of* the Holy.

This was my focus when I was asked to give the opening words for the worship service that marks the annual Professional Day of the Unitarian Universalist Ministers Association, in which twenty-five- and fifty-year-old memories are offered as sermons. "We are the prayer" kept repeating itself in my mind, so I began, "Let us create a prayer together." I spoke of individuals who create the community, of their meeting, of their relating, and of their eventual dispersing, and their prayerful nature. The prayer, "Let Us Create a Prayer Together," grew out of these elements. To emphasize our joint creation of the prayer, I repeated each line of the prayer as it was developing until it was complete. "Spirit of Life and Love, where we meet is a sacred space and we are inspired by one another's presence. At the center of the gathered community dwells the Holy. We are the prayer, each and all. We are the prayer, each and all. Amen." The prayer has subsequently been used (that I know of) to bless the gathering at a building dedication and an ordination, attesting to its broad application.

Sometimes the strongest way we can say something is to acknowledge its opposite. If we are joyful, we can contrast it with the times we have been filled with despair. When we are hopeful, our hope is lifted up by naming the times we have been without hope. The most loving way to mourn a death is to celebrate the life that preceded it, sometimes letting laughter be a prelude to tears. When we turn the tables on the ordinary, we often find extraordinary riches beneath it.

This is what prompted me to create a Thanksgiving Day prayer in 1999, "Gratitude For What We May Take For Granted," listing the things we take for granted and offering them as misplaced gratitude. This kind of turning things around works well for annual events, celebrations that tend to get stagnant with assumptions. "We are not ungrateful— not all the time. We know that life is a most precious gift. Though we would appear at times to squander it, remember the ways we do not."

PRAYING TOGETHER

EVERY FAITH TRADITION HAS AT LEAST one familiar form of address that sets a tone for private or denominational prayer. Such familiarity offers instant recognition of who and where you are and provides a sense of comfort to that tradition's worshipers.

Often, the form of address is suggested by the tradition's sacred writings. Hence, the Muslim speaks directly to Allah; the Jew to Adonai, Jehovah, or Yahweh; the Christian to Father, Lord, Jesus, or Christ. There are hundreds of permutations and formulas within each tradition.

Yet this is where the excluding often begins in public prayer. To one outside a particular faith, a specific name can sound foreign or abusive. To many women, and to all who believe the Holy has no gender, a masculine address such as

"Father" offers a counter-image to what is held in the heart. Worshipers whose traditions are based on the democratic process find references such as "King" or "Lord" to be troubling. And to people who name themselves agnostic or atheist—people I have often found to be very spiritual in their approach to religious questing—even the designation "God" can set off negative vibrations. Fortunately, "God" is not God's name or title, and we are free to look beyond the familiar in our prayers.

If we begin any communication with a negative-producing concept, what follows has less chance of being heard. So it stands to reason that if you want your prayer to be heard by those among whom you are praying—as far as I know, the Spiritual Addressee is not nearly so sensitive to naming as we, and will accept most any form or title—you want to begin with something that will include everyone. It is useful when writing a prayer to formulate your address to the known group(s) in attendance, or to the topic of the meeting in which the prayer is set.

Early on, when creating prayers for wedding ceremonies, I hit upon the formula, "Spirit of Life and Love ..." It offends no one and speaks to two very important concepts of theological thought in keeping with the wedding ceremony. When I look back on the written record of my own prayers, this is the form of address I find I have used most often. Even we non-traditionalists can fall into using habitual phrases, when thoughtful creativity would be more helpful. Fortunately, there are other people's examples from which to choose.

Rev. Norm Naylor began his prayer for a Community Interfaith Prayer Breakfast in this manner: "God of many names: Jehovah, Yahweh, Allah, The One, The Tao, Spirit of Life, God our Father and God our Mother, come to us all and be a vital presence in the work of all communities of faith." Throughout this prayer, "God of Many Names," Naylor continued to name the diverse communities present as a way of being specifically inclusive.

Taking a more minimalist approach, Rev. Greta Crosby left it up to the participants to supply their own names for the Holy in her opening prayer, "To Honor Our Diversity," for a Yakima, Washington, Interfaith Coalition annual meeting. Only then did she offer metaphorical examples of her own. "Honoring the diversity of our spiritual heritages and the unity of our human condition, I invite you silently to call upon what is highest and deepest by the name you hold sacred and dear." Again at the end of the prayer, Greta allowed each participant to address his or her own God in closing.

On the occasion of a World AIDS Day Celebration, in her prayer "Celebration of Life," Rev. Jonalu Johnstone chose to address a creator God, one who gives life and takes it away. This form of address fit with the theme of the celebration even as it remained inclusive to all in attendance: "Oh Life that loves us into being, we love you, Life, and we celebrate the gifts you bring to us."

Here are a few more brief examples of addressing the Holy in an inclusive manner:

"Dear Holy and infinite Source of love, mercy, justice and right-eousness"
— REV. SUSAN SUCHOCKI BROWN, "To Serve the Good of All"

"Spirit of life, in whose image we are both male and female"
— REV. LAUREL HALLMAN, "On Women Who Dream"

"O God of our Being and Becoming"
— REV. PRISCILLA RICHTER, "On a New Year"

"Infinite and Ultimate Mystery, you are called by many names: God, Yahweh, Wankantaka, Allah, Brahman, Goddess, Sat Nam, Creative Interchange, Void, Ahura Mazda, Ground of Being"
— REV. DR. VERN BARNETT, "Joined in Public Service"

•   •   •

When we pray together, we have to ask, "Who else is listening?" The answer, of course, is the gathered community with whom we are praying. There are times, then, when we won't address the Holy, except by reference, but will pray addressing the congregants—the worldly listeners—or the purpose and sub-ject matter of the meeting itself. This latter technique is highly effective when the work being honored by the public gathering is considered worthy of sacred attention.

A secular start to a prayer—that is, one that makes no overt mention of a Higher Power—has the affect of engaging and involving the community. It says, "This is important to us." It says, "You are important to the work we do." It says, "Something important is happening here."

Rev. Mark Allstrom began his invocation for a rededication of an interfaith chapel, "May Their Need Be Answered," by reminding people why they were there. In doing so, he drew the community into the holy work and the Holy into the community: "We come in the spirit of love and caring. We come here to open our spirits to the Great Spirit. We come here to open our souls to the Oversoul. We come here to dedicate this chapel to all that is holy and to give thanks to our God."

Rev. Beth Graham, in "Courage, Compassion, Commitment," an invocation for a legislative meeting, addressed the participants, stressing the fact that they came from separate places, with their own skills and attitudes:

> From different places you have arrived this morning.
> You have gathered here, both women and men:
> as eighteen individuals with eighteen disparate life
>   paths, vocations and avocations;
> as people from differing homes from various corners
>   of our great county;

as people from different political parties holding an array of guiding life values.

Having set the stage, she suggested that each individual invoke three guides essential to his or her work—courage, compassion, and commitment. Her prayer returns to this theme over and over again, supporting the work being done.

There are many ways of addressing the Holy by inference, while invoking the gathered community. In an invocation ("To Hear One Another") before a labor association council meeting in Washington state, I suggested that hearing one another was indeed the sacred work of us all. I suggested ways we might accomplish this sacred hearing:

> Listen, listen carefully…
> The beating of our own hearts calls us to ourselves…
> The breath of our neighbor calls us outside
> ourselves…

With the suggestion that we all receive the call to do good works, I ended the prayer as I began it, with an exhortation to *listen.*

Because she lives in an area with a large Hispanic population, Rev. Susan Manker-Seale took the opportunity to invite participants at an interfaith vigil and memorial service to listen to one another by offering her opening prayer in two languages: "Night of Martyrs, Dawn of Hope (*Noche de Martires, Amanecer de Esperanza*)." She invites listeners in both English and Spanish to be present and to join with one another "hand in hand" (*mano a mano*); and "heart to heart" (*corazon a corazon*). To be inclusive, we can learn to speak another language, whether it is an actual language or the language of faith.

Although Rev. Calvin Dame began his invocation, "Remembering Our Virtues," to the Maine House of Representatives with the traditional "Spirit of Life and Love," he was really addressing the representatives. In his prayer, he asks for their gratitude, responsibility, perspective, inspiration, and memory. The Holy may be called into partnership with them, but it is the representatives themselves to whom he is speaking and to whom he attempts to bring inspiration and hope. Dame begins each exhortation with similar words, "May this day we be...," lending the prayer the tone of a litany. This repetition builds a mounting sense of urgency and importance, until he ends with: "And may the members of this House maintain a high sense of their calling, remember that they are invested here with honor and called to a wider vision of the world, a world made more fair, more just, more equitable by their efforts."

Finally, there are instances when the Holy is invoked by implication as you speak directly to those in whom the Holy resides. Such an instance is found in the "Prayer for the Blessing and Dedication of Animals," offered annually in my own congregations. Before the blessing, each person who has brought a pet—photographs and stuffed toys are encouraged as surrogates—is given real or symbolic food for the animal. Before asking the humans in each relationship to offer the food and a blessing to their pet(s), a prayer is said that speaks directly to the cats, dogs, snakes, turtles, rabbits, mice, gerbils, birds, and other pets assembled (twice there were ponies, and once, a llama): "My furry, feathered, and scaled friends, I greet you. You come from the same Life Force of Creation that I do, and I greet you as a sister." The human participants give the actual blessing.

Problems with inclusion become apparent at the end of a traditional, faith-bound public prayer as often as they do at the beginning. How do you sign off on a prayer without offending someone? Rev. Kathleen McTigue often uses the simple phrase, "Let us worship together." Rev. Eileen Karpeles ends an invocation with: "So be it forever and ever, days without end." In Sunday morning services, I always end the benediction with: "So may it be in your lives."

The increase in some circles of pagan-based celebrations has made the ending "Blessed Be!" familiar, but it can be as offensive to a non-pagan as "In Jesus' name we pray" is to a non-Christian. Some ministers solve the problem by using a double or triple sign-off: "Amen. So be it. Blessed Be!" I often invite the celebrating community into the spirit of worship by asking them to speak the endings with me. I did this, for example, in "We All Speak" at an ordination in Bellevue, Washington, in 1992; after asking for the shared voices of the congregation in the introduction of the prayer, I concluded: "In this we all speak, saying 'Amen.' Amen. In this we all speak, saying, 'Blessed Be!' Blessed Be!"

There doesn't have to be a traditional ending at all. You might finish your prayer with instructions for continuing to maintain the sacred space, as I did in "What Can Save Us?" at an interfaith Thanksgiving service, saying, "Go in gratitude for the gifts of Life and Love. Go in appreciation for the presence of one another. Go as thankful people to tempt the world to joy." The important thing is to be aware of and sensitive to your audience.

I can't talk about ending prayers without commenting on the tendency of some pray-ers to go on and on and on. It's as if, when we have the ear of the Holy, we simply have to tell everything we know or need. When I am listening to another's prayer, I sometimes find myself thinking, "That would have been a good place to stop." Perhaps it's the age-old problem first noted by Mark Twain: "It takes longer to write a short piece than it does a long one." Any time is a good time for a short prayer, in my opinion, but the time when brevity is of the essence is in the grace before meals (especially when the food is hot and on the table).

It is helpful to study those colleagues who have mastered the art of brevity, noting that a lot can be said in few words.

●　●　●

Creatively saying goodbye at the end of an event can be as important and challenging as crafting the prayer itself. The speakers have spoken, the prayers have been said, the work is done. How do we take leave of one another? How we disperse our community is as important as why we gathered it. We need a spiritual good-bye to one another before we go.

In a public setting, especially when good work has been done or when the community has been gathered successfully for a long period of time, I have found that a formal leave-taking ceremony eases the tension of personal good-byes. I've also found that it's alright to cry in public, and that has made saying farewell less traumatic for me.

For a District Religious Education Conference, I used a line from Omar Khayyam, "I came like Water, and like Wind I go." For the opening prayer, "Go Like the River," I used the metaphor of water, and for the closing, wind. "And the wind is in the breath of our being, in the words of our telling, in the memory of our passing."

At the end of a week at a Winter Institute, I created a responsive reading that allowed everyone to participate in saying good-bye. The metaphor this time was the body: just as our bodies have many parts that do specialized work, so does the body of a conference have many specialists. We closed the litany, "Separate, Yet Joined by Common Purpose," saying, "We are the members and the body. When we are separate, may we be as one; as we go forth, may we be united."

Probably the most successfully inclusive prayers are those created communally. The members of the Muslim community of Dayton, Ohio, joined with the Unitarian Universalist churches recently to celebrate their common goals and build closer ties. As part of their meeting, they jointly created "A Litany of Faith and Hope" to end their shared worship. The prayer began, "We are a garden." The rest of the group responded, "A community of many different varieties growing together, we need water, sun, and soil. We have one source. We live alongside one another, respecting one another, maintaining our identities, like an iris and a carnation." The prayer ends with all saying, "The world is big enough for all of us. So may it be in all our lives."

PRAYERS

UNITY AND DIVERSITY

Let Us Create a Prayer Together

LET US CREATE A PRAYER TOGETHER:

At the center of the gathered community dwells the Holy. We are the prayer, each and all.

One by one, we come to this place—whole and broken, commencing and concluding, laughing and weeping. And soul by soul the prayer begins. "Spirit of Life and Love ..."

Two by two, we greet one another—smiling, nodding, speaking, embracing. And in relationship, the prayer continues. "Spirit of Life and Love, where we meet is a sacred space ..."

Moment by moment the circle builds, pulsing like four hundred heartbeats. We fill the circle with our breath; we inspire. The circle fills us with wealth; we are inspirited. The prayer rises on our very breathing together. "Spirit of Life and Love, where we meet is a sacred space and we are inspired by one another's presence ..."

This circle will not, cannot, go on forever, yet this circle will never die. What each of us finds here is what we are not. It makes us whole. It gives us strength to go out in the world beyond this holy community, beyond this sacred space, to begin yet another prayer. Let us pray:

"Spirit of Life and Love, where we meet is a sacred space and we are inspired by one another's presence. At the center of the gathered community dwells the Holy. We are the prayer, each and all. We are the prayer, each and all. *Amen.*"

—L. ANNIE FOERSTER
opening words, Unitarian Universalists Ministers' Association
annual worship service

Prayer of Presence

AS WE HAVE EACH BEEN BLESSED in our lives by the gifts
and the giving of others,
let us reach out now.

Reach out and touch those near you –
    clasp a hand,
    touch a shoulder,
    link an arm.
Make this community of being, which we together *are*,
    now tangible.
    Feel it.
    It is real.
    We are real.
    We are here.
    We are now.
    We can never be anywhere else.
So what we withhold from this moment,
    we withhold from ourselves and from the world.
What we deny in this moment,
    we deny to ourselves and to Life.
And only what we give do we ever get to keep.
So, dear friends, let us live into our dreams,
    and make them as real as we are.
Let us *become* them,
    so that we ourselves are a gift and a giving.
Amen.

—Margaret Keip

Aren't We All One Family?

Spirit of Ages, Light of Life,

We gather this evening from many traditions and many ways of life to speak with one strong voice—to give thanks and to worship together.

Let our prayer be heard, for aren't we all one family, with the same wants and needs? Help us to strive for a healthy planet; to work toward peaceful, loving relationships with all of humankind; to achieve our vision of seeing all people fed in body and nourished in soul, sheltered from the rain, and free from unnecessary fears.

Let our thanks be heard, for aren't we all one family, with the same joys and sorrows? Hear our praise of love and beauty; accept our gratitude for the promise of children; harken to our songs of celebration—for music, for learning, for the solid earth beneath our feet, and for the clear distant sky above, we offer thanks.

Let our efforts be forever intertwined, for aren't we all one family, gathered here this night, together, grateful for the warmth and recognition we find in one another's hearts and faces?

Thus we pray, and thus we offer thanks, and thus we love. So be it. *Amen.*

—L. Annie Foerster
Thanksgiving invocation

Meditation on Listening

I OFFER YOU THE WORD, "Listen." Listen. Listen. Listen to the sounds of the sanctuary that surrounds you. Sounds that surround you now. Sounds that have surrounded you in other services, in other activities, in other moments of quiet, in other moments of joy. Listen to the quiet. Especially the quiet.

Listen. Listen to the voice within that speaks of the sanctity of this place. Listen to the voices of those around you, voices of relationship. What are those voices telling you about yourself? Listen.

When you are through listening to the voice within, the voices without, then open your eyes and live with awareness.

—SUSAN M. WOLINSKY

To Hear One Another

The ringing of a bell calls us to worship.
  The pounding of a drum calls us to war.
  The popping of a cork calls us to celebration.
    What is the sound that calls us to hear one another?
Listen ... Listen carefully ...
  It is here, in the silence ... Listen deeply ...

The beating of our own hearts calls us to ourselves;
> calls us to be our true selves;
> calls us to be our best selves;
> calls us to be what we might become.

Listen … There is another sound …
> The breath of our neighbor calls us outside ourselves;
> > calls us to be companions;
> > calls us to be allies;
> > calls us to be partners.

Listen … we must heed the call of our own hearts,
> where love and truth, caring and justice, are born.

Listen … we must heed the call of others,
> to gather together for some great purpose,
> where passion and fidelity, compassion and equity, are nourished.

The hammering silence calls us together
> that we may do the work we cannot do alone.

Let us heed the calls that come in the silence,
> that we may be well,
> and do good,
> in this world together. *Amen.*

—L. ANNIE FOERSTER

The Interdependent Web

WHENEVER LIFE LOOKS EASY,
    know that it is more complex than it seems.
The simplest, most profound pieces of art
    have exquisite planning.
The melody line rises to the surface
    because it has been played out
    in the composer's mind
    and the notes arranged and rearranged
    until all the intricate connections
    are designed for clarity.
We see the web, the end result,
    strung on the front porch in the morning sun.
We did not see the tireless spinning and weaving through
    the night,
    the near miss of the bat's flight
    or the casual brush with the cat's evening prowl along
    the rail.
And what we think we see is much less than what lives in
    the depths.
There is always more than what meets the eye.

And so we ask for patience,
    when we would wish for everything to be clear.

We ask for insight,
when we can see no further than our own needs.
We give forgiveness when others
look into our lives
and see no deeper than the surface
of themselves reflected there;
And we are humbled when we find we do little better
and seek ourselves in others as well.
In the quiet we reach inward to that still place.

—ELIZABETH O'SHAUGHNESSY BANKS

A Litany of Faith and Hope

LEADER: We are a garden:
ALL: A community of many different varieties growing
together,
we need water, sun, and soil.
We have one source.
We live alongside one another, respecting one another,
maintaining our identities,
like an iris and a carnation.
LEADER: We come together:
ALL: To discover we have a common language:
our children.

our families.

LEADER: We seek:

ALL: To know one another.

LEADER: We need:

ALL: To build on these experiences of community,
to be full of care for people of all faiths.

We believe in our children being friends with other children
who may not look like them, who may hold different
beliefs, who have different backgrounds.

We believe the barriers are in our minds; justice, peace, and
understanding will ultimately prevail.

We believe we share a common origin as human beings; we
are children of the same creator.

We believe in the dignity and worth of all human beings.

We know the world is big enough for all of us.

—*members of the Moslem and Unitarian Universalist*
Communities of Greater Dayton, Ohio

Together in Love

LET US BE

Let us be together

Let us be together in love

    in respect

in honor

in appreciation

in wonder

in joy

Let us be together in harmony

Let us be together with unity

with peace

with hope

with charity

with compassion

with justice

with mercy

Let us be together with gladness for all that makes us human,
striving to be and become more than we are,

to become more human, more merciful, justice-seeking
and loving.

Fill us with the spirit of all heroes and heroines, saints and
saviors, named and unnamed,

and fill us with the spirit of Martin, in whose name we
are gathered this day,

whose name means justice, unity, compassion, courage,
vision and hope.

Fill us with his spirit of love, of hope, of justice.

Let us be

Let us be together this day and all the days to come.
Blessed Be.

—SUSAN SUCHOCKI BROWN
Martin Luther King, Jr. celebration

We Are Woven Together

WE GATHER TODAY AS A DIVERSE body of people from
many faiths and traditions.
We do not speak the same language of worship.
We follow different teachings,
made known to us by sacred voices and scriptures
through the ages.
We do not utter the same prayers,
nor do we even use the same word, if any word at all,
to speak the name of God.
Nevertheless, we gather together in worship.
In our gathering, we honor and celebrate our diversity.
We do not seek a unity that would deny our differences.
We seek rather a deeper union, a union woven through
choice and intent,
through time and attention,
through respect and compassion,

until we recognize that we have become a whole cloth,
   a cloth made rich and textured and vibrant through our
   differences.
Each of us can hear, in the beating of our own hearts,
   the ancient rhythm of the loom at work.
We are woven together.
We are bound to one another.
We belong to and with each other.
Let us worship together.

—KATHLEEN MCTIGUE
Interfaith Alliance chapter meeting

Let Me Tell You Who We Are

SPIRIT OF AGES, CREATOR OF LIFE and Love, whose names and attributes are infinite, knowable and unknown; oh, Spirit, hear our prayers. Our names, too, are many. Let me tell you who we are.

We are those who are innocent and those who are wise. We are those who are proud and those who are humble. We are those who are accepted and those who are shunned without understanding why.

We are those who love life and those who are fearful and confused. We are those who know abundance and those who know scarcity. We are inheritors of the past and architects of the future. We are givers and we are receivers.

We are larger than our skins and smaller than our egos. We are diversity incarnate, dressed in all the glorious hues of ethnicity and all the fascinating textures of genetics. We are the harvests of creation, related by our humanity and separated only by our own voices. We seek a common language, a language of love.

Ancient One, it is important to know us in our rich diversity, for we struggle to know ourselves and one another. Wise One, it is important to know us in our myriad similarities, for we are forgetful and need reminding. Dear One, it is important to know us in our many disguises, for we need but one thing: Help us to love; and help us to know we are worthy of love. In this we are as one. *Amen.*

—L. ANNIE FOERSTER
gay pride service

Celebration of Life

OH LIFE THAT LOVES US INTO BEING,
    we love you, Life, and we celebrate the gifts you
    bring to us:
        the splendor and terror of the storm,
        the breathless moment just before dawn,
        the stunning variety of life, both delicate and strong.
We came into being from Love,
    embracing life with passion,
    living in bodies, both vulnerable and strong.
Living this fragile life, we have seen the tragedy of AIDS,
    men and women reduced to skeletal selves, only to
        finally die;
    children robbed of their entire lives.
Our hearts and minds are with all of those whose lives are
    gone.
We have felt the tragedy of AIDS,
    some of us in our own bodies, others in our souls.
Our hearts and minds are with all of those throughout the
    world infected with the virus.
We can envision the tragedy of AIDS—what it can become,
    if not stopped
    through prevention, education, research, and treatment.

Our hearts and minds are with all of those who fight the
     hard and seemingly endless fight.
May we find the hope and comfort we need to continue
     whatever challenges and trials lie before us.
May we find peace whatever chaos surrounds us.
So may it be for all of us.

— JONALU JOHNSTONE
World AIDS Day

The Issues That Divide Us

SPIRIT OF LOVE,

So many of the issues that divide us exist only in our
minds, created from our misconceptions and misunderstand-
ings. May we look with the eyes of spirit and the eyes of heart
to see beyond the barriers we built to cloak our fears, and the
monuments we erected to celebrate our foolishness. These
are our prayers of diversity:

Let the colors of our skin be seen as richly hued paints
on the canvas of humanity. We shall not allow the variety of
our experiences, the unique traditions of our families, nor
the genetics of our birth to be diminished by the false epi-
thet of race.

Let the inspirations of our affections be seen as manifest ways of expressing love. We shall not allow the physical assumptions of bodies, the mistaken injustices of the past, nor the brutal ignorance of prejudice to denigrate the inner knowledge of our gendering.

Let the patterns of our lives be seen as ever-changing rivers, whose shores create rich landscape and whose common destination is the great ocean of life. We shall not allow the dictates of fashion, the presumption of numbers, nor the fear of death to belittle the accumulation of our years.

Fear and foolishness will fade away when the spirit is set free. So let it be for you; so let it be for me. *Amen.*

—L. ANNIE FOERSTER

Knitted Together by Music

BEING MEMBERS OF THE HUMAN RACE, of the family of
woman and man,
and longing for better family relations,
we have gathered as one this afternoon.
Having eyes of knowledge that can no longer not see
the good and evil that surround us,
we have gathered as one this afternoon.

Knitted together by so many strands of music,
from so many different religious and ethnic communities—
        their rhythmic measures still stirring our souls—
                we have gathered as one this afternoon.
Inspired by words from the lips of five remarkable young
        people,
moved by given messages that are far more honest and
        direct than
many of those uttered by people two or three or four or even
        five times these students' ages—
                we have gathered as one this afternoon.
In the name of all that is within us
        that can dream a better world,
and all that is within us
        that can help shape such a home,
                we have gathered as one today.
Thanks be for this gathering.

—BETH GRAHAM
First Harmony Concert of Anti-Bias Task Force

Night of Martyrs, Dawn of Hope
(Noce de Martires, Amanecer de Esperanza)

LET US JOIN HEARTS in the spirit of meditation and prayer:

Juntemos los corazones en el espiritu de meditacion y oracion:

Mysterious Presence,

Presencia misteriosa,

God, our Father and our Mother,

Dios, nuestro Padre y nuestra Madre,

Spirit of Life whom we struggle to name in our joys and our
   sorrows,

*Espiritu de la Vida a quien nos esforzamos nombrar dentro los deleites y las
   penas,*

let Your presence be known

dejanos sentir a Tu presencia

through the breath that feeds our words,

por el aliento que alimenta nuestra palabras.

Let Your presence be known

Dejanos sentir a Tu presencia

through the beat of our hearts in the rush of caring.

por las palpitaciones de nuestros corazones dentro la pasion del carino.

Let Your presence be known

Dejanos sentir a Tu presencia

through the warmth of our hands as we reach out to one
   another in faith and hope.

*por el calor de las manos mientras que alcanzamos el uno al otro en fe y
esperanza.*

Hand in hand,

Mano a mano,

heart to heart,

corazon a corazon,

breaths mingled in one cry for Justice,

alientos mezclados en un vocerio por las Justicia,

one shout for Liberty,

un grito por la Libertad,

one song for Peace,

una cancion por la Paz,

we shall bring forth the dawn of a world community that
balances all the best of Life,

*daremos a luz el amanecer de una comunidad mundial que equilibra todo
lo mejor de la vida.*

This night of martyrs,

Esta noche de martires,

we come together,

nos juntamos,

the Dawn of Hope.

el Amanecer de Esperanza.

We will have a moment of silence to be with our own
thoughts and prayers.

Habra un momento de silencio para que estemos solos con nuestros propio
   pensamientos
y con nuestras porpias oraciones.
[Silence/*Silencio*]
Breath with breath, heart to heart, hand in hand.
Aliento con alineto, corazon a corazon, mano a mano.
Amen.
Amen.

—SUSAN MANKER-SEALE
interfaith vigil and memorial service

To Honor Our Diversity

HONORING THE DIVERSITY of our spiritual heritages and the
unity of our human condition, I invite you silently to call upon
what is highest and deepest by the name you hold sacred and
dear. [Pause.]

Spirit of life and love, mover of the compassionate heart
and human mind, melder of community, be present to us as
we gather in celebration and in endeavor. May we be alight
with your fire in all our works.

We welcome the many presences here, each person
uniquely formed and still forming in life's crucible, each one
in turn a gift and a giver to the world.

[Here Rev. Crosby inserted specific thanks for things that had happened in the past.]

Creating, sustaining, renewing spirit, be with us today in our glad greetings, in our heartfelt thanksgivings, and in our bittersweet farewells. Be with us as we seek to embody your love in all our works. Be with us now and always.

Now I invite each of us to silently add a word of our own to the one who hears. [Pause.]

And now let us bring our meditation or prayer to a close, each in our own way.

So be it. *Amen.*

— GRETA CROSBY
Interfaith Coalition annual meeting

God of Many Names

GOD OF MANY NAMES: Jehovah, Yahweh, Allah, The One, the Tao, Spirit of Life, God our Father and God our Mother, come to us all and be a vital presence in the work of all the community of faith. Be present in them as they work to strengthen in their members the sense of your presence in their lives. Be with us as each of our communities of faith, in its own way, tries to discern the direction of your will that we may aspire to some Ultimate Creative Good, here and in the world, in which you and we move, and have our being.

Be present in our churches, temples, synagogues, and mosques as together we work to strengthen the eternal values of all of us—the values of life and kindness and justice. Move in us as we care for and about this city, that it may more perfectly be a place for all to live and work in safety and neighborliness.

God of many names, work through us as justice, that we may feed the hungry and clothe the naked, for even here is the presence of injustice and the need for redress.

Come to our entire community of many faiths as a voice of conscience and caring, a voice urging us to prevent the kind of evil that has destroyed lives and shattered families elsewhere.

God of many names, come to us as value and respect for our different faith, for the diversity of faith that is natural, and for the numerous ways by which we invoke your presence in our congregations and in our personal lives.

Be present in our communities of faith as a vision of the oneness of all the human family—that all of us are in your image—that all of us are moved by the force of your presence within us—that all of us need the same things in order to live full lives that honor you.

Help each of our faith communities to fulfill its mission;
to do its work more perfectly; to make the world and our city
a better place for its presence.

God of many names, come to us, be with us, move us in
the ways of lovingkindness, peace, and justice. *Amen.*

—NORM NAYLOR
community prayer breakfast

Out of Our Yearning

WE SPEAK TO THE GOD, the goddess, the spirit of life, the
    eternal.
We speak to the mysterious thread that connects us one to
    the other and to the universe.
We speak to the deep wisdom at the center of our beings.
We embody the yearning of all people
    to touch each other more deeply,
    to hear each other more keenly,
    to see each other's joys and sorrows as our own
    and know that we are not alone,
    unless we create solitude for ourselves;
    and even then, community awaits us.
Out of our yearning we have come
    to this religious community.

May we help each other to proclaim the possibilities we see,
    to create the community we desire,
    to worship what is worthy in our lives,
    to teach the truth as we know it,
    and to serve with justice in all the ways that we can,
    to the end that our yearning is assuaged
    and our lives fulfilled in one another.
Let us go, now, into the silence of the faith that is
    unique to each of us, and still the same.
Let us be silent together for a moment.
    [Pause.]
May peace be yours.

—SUSAN MANKER-SEALE
invocation for an interfaith worship

Unite Us

O THOU WHO MADE US one nation out of many people, amidst our diversities of race and tradition and faith, unite us in a common love of freedom. Revive in us a spirit of devotion to the common good, so that we may open new doors to the neglected and oppressed. Cleanse the heart of our nation from that greed which preys upon others. Endow our leaders with wisdom, that we may stand among nations as an example of benevolence and exalted justice. Help us to make this land a common workshop of its people, where all may find their place and work, keen to do their best.

Hear these words of the Athenian, Pericles: "I would have you day by day fix your eyes upon the greatness of your country, until you become filled with love for her; and when you are impressed by the spectacle of her glory, reflect that it has been acquired by men and women who knew their duty and had the courage to do it."

And these words of the Hebrew Psalmist: "Let the people give praise, O God of all the nations."

—JOHN BUEHRENS

Prayer for Patience

SOMEWHERE AT OUR INNERMOST core, each of us wants to submerge self-interest so that we may do that which is right: to promulgate justice tempered by mercy. But this is not always an easy path for human, all-too-fallible men and women. Knowing this, we ask tonight for patience, that we may diligently weigh conflicting evidence and find the right therein. We ask for tolerance, that we may truly hear *and consider* opinions unlike our own. We ask for wisdom, that we may recognize the face of truth when it appears before us.

All this we ask in the name of that eternal creative Spirit,
that supreme power, that guides all of us, whatever our traditions, to act in ways that are loving, wise, and just.

So be it, forever and ever, days without end.

—EILEEN KARPELES
city council invocation

Joined in Public Service

INFINITE AND ULTIMATE MYSTERY,
The Citizens of Kansas call you by many names—
God, Yahweh, Wankantaka, Allah, Brahman, Goddess, Sat Nam,
Creative Interchange, Void, Ahura Mazda, Ground of Being—
These names planted and transplanted here, the great
traditions of the world now growing in our own garden.

We are joined as a sunflower is joined with the plains while
it reaches upward beyond itself.
We are joined as the rivers and streams are joined as they
travel to the oceans of the planet.
We are joined as the eagle is joined with the sky.
So are we joined in this chamber with the citizens on whose
behalf we hold offices of trust,

and joined with the past and future as we live together
    honoring you as the Eternal Spirit of Service.

You, who from ancient times has joined us in shapes like
    covenant, compact, and constitution, as the means by
    which we may co-create a humane, educated, and
    prosperous society,
You, Spirit of Generations, bless all those here and
    everywhere serving the public weal in many ways.
On this new day, accept us anew as we join again with the
    calls to stewardship,
liberty, justice, righteousness, and love. *Amen.*

—VERN BARNETT
Kansas House of Representatives invocation

Help Us to Do Our Best

OUT OF OUR OCCUPATIONS AND PREOCCUPATIONS,
from the homes and churches that ask of us so much,
we have come here to this place.

Now, in the season of the growing dark,
in the season of buying and wrapping and shipping and
    planning,

the season of pageant rehearsals and recalcitrant choirs,
from the midst of all this,
with our suitcases and our plane tickets and our half-
   finished sermons,
we have come here to this place.

This place, which stands as a beacon
to all who treasure the life of the mind,
to all who would offer intelligent service to a troubled world,
to all who would preserve the heritage of freedom, thought,
   and devotion—
which is our liberal religious tradition.

Into our hands it is now given to shape the future of this place:
to chart, as best we may,
a course of honor and health and fruitfulness for it
amid the chances and challenges of the world it would serve.

This task calls for our best, most thoughtful,
and most centered selves.
In such spirit, let us pray:
O Thou whose endless creativity delights to be expressed
in the endeavor of human hearts and minds,
bless the deliberations of this assembly
with intentions of righteousness,

with candid and amiable tone,
and with a productive tension between prudence and daring.

Be with us as we seek to build a school
that may worthily contribute to Thy purposes
of love and justice in this world. *Amen.*

—KENDYL GIBBONS
board of trustees invocation at Meadville/Lombard Theological School

When We Are Strongest

WE WHO SERVE IN OUR own congregations, separated from one another, are reminded by our meeting here together, and by our taking of food together, that we work within an unseen company who share our vocation. May we be reminded by our common meal that we are strongest when we strengthen one another and that we are capable of inspiring others better when we inspire one another.

So may we be worthy of this food and the cause we serve. *Amen.*

—ROBERT SENGHAS
grace for interfaith ministers' meeting

Go Like the River

LIKE WIND I GO
With them the Seed of Wisdom did I sow,
And with mine own hand wrought to make it grow;
    And this was all the Harvest that I reap'd—
"I came like Water, and like Wind I go."

—OMAR KHAYYAM,
trans. Edward Fitzgerald

WE CAME LIKE WATER AND like wind we go. And the wind is
in the breath of our being, in the words of our telling, in the
memory of our passing. Before we go, I would like to offer a
blessing. When you hear a phrase that begins "blessed be,"
please repeat the phrase as a response.

We have breathed this air together just as we have shared
food and space and fellowship. These are small personal
winds, individual winds of our own creation, but they signal
our existence to one another. "Blessed be these winds of our
lives."

We have told our words, one to the other—the wind of
our lips transporting the sound to distant ears. These are
winds of reason, of question, of knowledge, and of caring.
Most especially these are winds of caring. Even as the winds
cease to blow, the echo of our words will be borne on other

winds, to other places and other times. These are winds of powerful force, for they are created in community. "Blessed be these winds of our sharing."

We leave this place as whirlwinds, blowing to our own corners of the earth, scattering the dry leaves of indifference, gathering the warm breath of friendship. We cannot see the winds, but we can see their work and will. "Blessed be these winds of our parting."

Go like the wind,
which has its start
at the center of things —
but has no end,
as life does not.
Life has within it movement
and purpose.
This movement is unceasing,
this purpose is unyielding.
Go. Go like the wind.
Amen.

— L. ANNIE FOERSTER
closing ceremony, religious education conference

Separate Yet Joined by Common Purpose

THE BODY OF THIS COMMUNITY is its members, distinct and recognizable entities, yet joined by common purpose and spirit. Some bonds remain, even as we prepare to separate; the body prevails when all of its separate parts perform. As we go on our ways—

We must use our eyes, that we may not be blind to what is going on about us.

> "My eyes shall be as cameras, turned upon the images of the world. Let me see with clarity, welcoming new visions without fear and attending to the familiar without assumption."

We must use our ears, that we may not be deaf to those who ask our help or offer to teach us.

> "My ears shall be as deep bowls, tuned to absorb the music of the spheres. Let me hear with precision the harshness as well as the harmonious, the cry as well as the coo, the complaint as well as the compliment."

We must use our minds, that we be not without understanding of what we see and hear.

> "My mind shall be as a mirror, placed upon the path of

perception and polished by use. Let me reflect without distortion, both inwardly and toward the world; let me observe and consider, engage and attend, comprehend and instruct; let me be wise enough to know when any of these are beyond my capacity."

We must use our tongues, that we may not be mute.

"My tongue shall be as a carillon whose voice is heard far and clear. Let me not stammer or be silent from fear of rejection, nor babble without soundness of idea; let me attain eloquence, avoiding soliloquy, diatribe and pedagogy."

We must use our hearts, that we may not falter.

"My heart shall be as a stone wrapped in velvet, as tender as it is strong, at once indomitable and impressible. Let me have courage, daring, and self-reliance, without neglecting tenderness, passion, and love."

We must use our hands, that our work may be done.

"My hands shall be an extension of all that I am. Let my fingers be sensitive to contact—touching, massaging, reassuring; give them strength to lift up, to support, to hold on; and let them help to create new ways of being in the world."

We must use our feet, that we may not stand still, nor falter, nor fall.

> "My feet shall be as pedestals and as propellers. Let me stand firm when foundation is required; let me lead on when guidance is needed; let me wend fearlessly when exploration is called for. May I step proudly, stride boldly, and stand strong, neither trampling, nor stumbling, nor tottering."

We are the members and the body.

> "When we are separate, may we be as one; as we go forth, may we be united."

— L. Annie Foerster
leave-taking ceremony

PEACE AND JUSTICE

Make Us Your Instruments of Peace

KINDLE IN OUR HEARTS, OH ETERNAL and loving God, gratitude for the memory of those who have gone before. Kindle
in our hearts, eternal and loving God, courage to face the
tragedies of life. Kindle wisdom to learn from the pains and
tribulations of the past, praying now so that we may learn
from our errors. Kindle strength in our hearts so that we may
be used to relieve oppression that too many endure. Kindle in
our hearts charity so that we may see the unity in everyone,
everyone across this grand and glorious world. Make us
instruments of Your Peace. Go now to become an instrument
of peace and the proud bearer of God's Glory. *Amen.*

—SUSAN SUCHOCKI BROWN
Veterans Day, Unity House for Veterans

Prayer for the Children

LET US PRAY IN THE NAME OF THE ONE, who is called by many names, the best of which is Love.

We pray for the children that:

In a world of waste, the waters of life may run clean and clear and quenching for them;

In a world of buying and getting, they may learn of the things without price or profit;

In a world where time flies, they may have time and place for being children and only children;

In a world of busyness, someone may have time to hold their hands across streets, hold them in their arms in times of tears, and hold them in their laps in times of quietness and stories.

In such a world, may the best that is in us, which is also named Love, move us to make our world of waste and getting and busyness and fleeting-time fit for them, that it may be, as we pray, a blessing and a benediction. *Amen.*

—MAX COOTS

On Public Service

GOD OF CREATION, WHOM WE try again and again to make into our own image, enable us to desire rightly and to be of use in the service of others. Be with this assembly in its work. Grant us the wisdom to create what is essential for the common good. Keep within each of our hearts a love for the cause of human welfare and a dedication to enrich the lives of all people. Guide us in our labor to maintain and strengthen our public lives. And remind us to be good stewards of the gift of life. *Amen.*

—BURTON CARLEY
opening session of Tennessee Recreation and Parks Association

On a New Year

O GOD OF OUR BEING AND BECOMING,

We enter a new year in the spirit of reflection: we look back to decisions made and issues we have dealt with, and we look ahead to the issues of the coming year, the decisions that we have yet to make. We ask you for wisdom; we ask you for strength in helping us to become better servants of your love. We take this time at the turning of the year to thank you for the gift of another year amidst the ridges and valleys of this beautiful city. We give thanks for the gift of life and for the abundance that is ours. May we always rejoice at the splendor of Creation.

On this evening we acknowledge issues that generate a lot of feelings. May you grant our public servants wisdom to make the decision that will bring the greatest good to the greatest number of people. We ask your blessing and guidance in this New Year.

We pray in the many names by which you are known. *Amen.*

—PRISCILLA RICHTER
city council invocation

Remembering Our Virtues

SPIRIT OF LIFE AND LOVE, which moves through us and
    through all the world ...
May we this day be grateful for the gift of life which is ours,
    remembering today and always that the life we have and
    hold is to us a mystery and precious.
May we this day be reminded of the responsibilities we carry,
    not so that we are intimidated or overwhelmed,
    but so that we may be true to them,

so that we may be faithful in carrying them forward.
May we this day maintain a sense of perspective,
  remembering who we are, engaging the tasks at hand,
  but understanding our limitations, understanding our
  own shortcomings,
  forgiving ourselves and others if we fall short of
  perfection.
May we this day be inspired, be filled with new breath,
  be filled with new enthusiasm,
  be ready to see fresh opportunity, new perspectives,
  unnoticed avenues for action and resolution.
And may we this day remember those virtues that bless our
  lives and bless the lives of others,
  the virtues of caring and concern,
  the virtues of honesty and respect,
  the virtues of charity, industry and patience.
And may the members of this House maintain a high sense
  of their calling,
  remember that they are invested here with honor
  and called to a wider vision of the world,
  a world made more fair, more just, more equitable, by
  their efforts.
Amen.

— CALVIN DAME

house of representatives invocation

Re-planting Hope with Our Prayers

CONSOLATION TO THE TROUBLED and grieving, hope to the despairing, liberation to the enslaved and freedom of the bound, hear our prayer, for we know nothing offers our world more hope than our worshiping together in peace, understanding, and love. Let that hope be planted and made to grow in your holy eternity.

America's soul drifts. Burned churches in the rural South are manifestations of our national pain. Let this, our response, become a microcosm of this illness's possible cure. Help us understand how its effectiveness depends upon our commitment to stop society from collapsing inward, through the realization articulated many years ago by Dr. Martin Luther King, Jr.: that we are all tied together in a single garment of destiny.

We pray together for praise and thanksgiving and for the giving of our gifts to help rebuild churches that have been burned and destroyed by the evil of hatred. Let our prayer help fashion a better and greater hope for the achievement of the realm of God. This we ask in the name of all that is holy. *Amen.*

— MARK ALLSTROM
ecumenical service to support Southern churches
destroyed by racist arson attacks

Keepers of the Dream

WHO ARE THE KEEPERS of the dream?

Good women and men of every race and nation who have
 suffered misfortune.

Who are keepers of the dream?

Those who act in harmony with nature and ban its
 despoliation.

Who are keepers of the dream?

Children and young people who act on love, caring, and
 understanding.

Who are keepers of the dream?

Those who work together for justice, fair and well-
 conceived, equitable for all.

And the nightmare of injustice?

When we fight and squabble, hate, fear, close others out.

And the continued legacy of nightmare?

Children who will carry the scars of neglect, abuse, poor
 education, malnutrition, and diminishing health care. The
 nightmare is men and women who suffer misfortune
 and have no help; those who ruthlessly use others or
 the world for selfish or thoughtless ends.

Now we are blessed and challenged this day to honor in
 renewal Martin Luther King.

This day only?

No! Every day I pray for courage and strength!

—GEORGE A. ROBINSON III

in memory of Rev. Martin Luther King, Jr.

Renewal of Our Spirit

NOW MAY THE SPIRIT THAT LEADS US in our search for
truth and justice—
that spirit that has impelled men and women to devote life
and fortune to public
service, beyond hope of fame or pull of pride—
may that spirit be alive and renewed in us now and
henceforth. *Amen.*

—ROBERT SENGHAS

benediction for public servants' meeting

A Rose Among Thorns

TWO YOUNG MOTHERS WERE VISITING together one summer
day and, while they conversed, their daughters played together in the backyard. Suddenly one of the girls came running in,
her face wet with tears.

"Oh, Mommy!" she wailed. "All of the roses in the garden out back have thorns!"

At the same moment, the other woman's daughter burst into the house, her face radiant and beaming with delight.

"Oh, Mommy!" she said with a smile. "Come out back with me and see! I've a wonderful discovery outside! There's a whole patch of thorn sticks in the backyard, and they all have beautiful rose flowers on top!"

This story is a parable that illustrates our most basic approach to the world. Our attitude toward life is shaped by our perspective on the world around us.

There are times when we must face the fact that the beauty of life is marred by the thorns of communal injustice, inequality, and indecency. There are also times when we must look beyond the thorns and focus our eyes on the flowers that transcend them.

As we dedicate today a precious addition to our zoo and our city—a Biblical garden for all to enjoy—let us pause to appreciate that this is a truly precious moment in life, a moment that manifests the appearance of love in the world as "a rose among thorns." In dedicating this spot, people of goodwill are joining hands to affirm our shared heritage, to make our world more beautiful, and, especially, to celebrate together the Golden Anniversary of the modern State of Israel. Could there possibly be a more fitting tribute than this

Garden of Peace, established for the good of all, to enhance our community?

In this spirit, we can appropriately recite these words hallowed by our tradition—a simple prayer that compels us to recognize the beauty in our midst and give thanks for it: "Blessed be you, O God, who has created the fragrances of plants."

—GARY P. ZOLA
Garden of Peace dedication

Let Us Learn Peace

(The prayer was written to be read by three people,
as indicated by the typefaces.)

PEACE IS MORE THAN THE ABSENCE OF WORRY.
It is the creation of safe havens for all;
It is the building of security for everyone;
It is the forgiveness of self, as well as one who would
harm you.

Let us seek contentment; let us learn peace.

Peace is more than the absence of discordance.

IT IS THE INTENT LISTENING TO DIVERSE POINTS OF VIEW;
IT IS THE INTENTIONAL SPEAKING OF ALL VOICES,
ONE AT A TIME;

IT IS THE TENSION WITHIN SILENCE THAT WELCOMES
ALL THOUGHTS.
Let us seek harmony; let us learn peace.
Peace is more than the absence of tension.
  It is studying the hard lesson of letting go;
  It is breathing through pain into tranquility;
  It is forming friendship out of enmity.
    LET US SEEK SERENITY; LET US LEARN PEACE.
    PEACE IS MUCH MORE THAN THE ABSENCE OF WAR.
It is observing the promised truce when anger would say, "no";
It is finding the just compromise when the ego would
say, "my way";
It is striving for reconciliation when the heart would say,
"revenge."
  Let us seek amity for all the earth; let us learn peace.

—L. ANNIE FOERSTER
Garden of Peace dedication

Prayer After a Riot

GOD OF JUSTICE, RECONCILIATION, AND LOVE,
  who stands with the oppressed,
  and who is to be found wherever human connection
  transcends human alienation:

We come before you this week baffled, contrite, in need and
in pain.
We confess the oppression that is part of our society,
abetted by our silent complicity.
We confess the subtle joy of seeing others act out our
hidden rage,
allowing us to keep our own angers suppressed.
We confess the ease with which we are distracted from
issues of fundamental justice,
by intellectual speculations about legal maneuvers or
news reporting techniques.
The fires of central Los Angeles ascend to you, O Holy One,
as evidence that we have no right to demand your mercy.
Yet we turn to you,
for human justice and human compassion seem so
unreachable
in this horrible moment.
Turn not away from us, O source of hope and healing,
but be with us in our pain.
Break our hearts, that we may know the hearts of those who
live in daily despair.
Sting our conscience until it is more trouble to sit in silent
complacency
than it is to speak out and demand change.

Take from us whatever we have that is the product of our
 brothers' and sisters' suffering.
All this we would give for the sake of living in a righteous
 land.
But give us also the strength for these sacrifices:
 renew our vision of the beloved community;
 open for us connections to those who fear and hate;
 and open our eyes to our common humanity.
Make us humble enough to acknowledge our own capacity
 to inflict pain,
 and draw us close enough to your love
 that we never act on those impulses.
Be with all the lost, the suffering, the bereaved, and the
 discontented;
 lead them into the path of genuine comfort and of
 productive anger.
Whirlwind of consequences and confrontation,
 however much we may deserve it,
 leave us not utterly bereft.
Sow the seeds of renewed dedication to simple justice,
 and make our hands your hands to hasten the day.
Amen.

— KENDYL GIBBONS
during the riots following the acquittal of police
accused of beating Rodney King in Los Angeles

After the Words and the Music and the Gathering

AFTER THE WORDS, A QUIET.
After the songs, the silence.
After the crowd has scattered, only the trampled grass
    recalls the gathering.
Peace and justice have need of you
    after the words and the music and the gathering.
God grant you the depth for dedication to justice.
God grant you the will to be a solitary apostle of peace.
    Amen.

—MAX COOTS
prayer at the close of a peace rally

Blessed Are the Just

BLESSED ARE THE JUST,
    for they have their reward in indestructible integrity.
Blessed are they who labor in the vineyards of the public realm,
    for they shall be remembered.
Blessed are they who love their nation enough to praise its
    strengths and criticize its weaknesses,
        for they shall be made wise.

Blessed are public officials who are responsive to the needs
     of these, the least of the people,
     for they shall be deputies of the community.
Blessed are they who serve the public good,
     for their reward is in being used.
Blessed are the powerful who acknowledge their power as
     both gift and responsibility,
     for they know the binding obligations of their bounty.
Blessed are they who rebuke narrow self-interest to sustain
     the commonweal,
     for they are the patriots the nation needs.
Blessed are they who rise above partisan loyalties,
     for they shall administer a public trust.
Blessed are all people who seek justice in an imperfect world,
     for they shall be welcomed into the Beloved Community.
                                        —RICHARD GILBERT

Prayer for Peace

THERE ARE ONE HUNDRED AND FIFTY of us here today.
One hundred and fifty uniquely personal faiths.
One hundred and fifty different understandings of God.
In this way we are not unlike this world—
     a world in which we invest our love and hope.

So let us invoke *love* and *hope*—attributes of God—
    and of ourselves, in reverence to that which is worthy.
Let us spend one whole and holy minute together in silent
    prayer,
    in which we each, true to our own faith,
    call forth within ourselves our *hope* or *love*. [Pause.]
Holding this reality close, may we become verbs,
May we *hope*.
May we *love*.
May we *do* peace, and make it real—
    make it our destiny, and make it *now*.
Amen.

—MARGARET KEIP

Courage, Compassion, Commitment

FROM DIFFERENT PLACES YOU HAVE arrived this morning.
You have gathered here, both women and men:
    as eighteen individuals with eighteen disparate life paths,
    vocations and avocations;
    as people from differing homes from various corners of
    our great county;
    as people from different political parties holding an array
    of guiding life values.

Different though you might be,

 you join together as one, each and every time you con-
 vene a legislative session such as this.
You join together as one, each and every time you speak up
 as a public body.
To prepare for the work that lies before you this day,
 might you begin your time together by invoking—
 by inviting in—
 three essential guides:

  courage; compassion; commitment.

It is by the will of God,

 it is from the hand of that which is the Most Holy
 (by whatever name we call this)
 that these three impulses dwell and grow within us.
In the name of all that is in you that has the courage to
 dream a healthier, less fragmented society—
In the name of all that is in you that has the compassion to
 notice the needs and vulnerabilities of many in our
 community, and all that is in you that moves your hearts
 and your hands to help soothe that distress—
In the name of all that is in you that has the commitment to
 believe that every single effort made on behalf of what-
 could-be matters—
In the name of all of this and more, you come together.
We begin this day, then, by bringing to the fore—

by inviting in—
by invoking—
all the courage, compassion, and commitment that
Creation has given you.
May your hearts and minds, too, be open to receiving even
more as you begin this day together,
as you ready yourselves for all the work that is etched
into your hearts,
into the lives of your constituents,
and into the written agenda that undoubtedly
are before you.
In a shared moment of silence, then, may you now invoke
for yourself—
may you invite in—
these three friends: courage; compassion, commitment.
[Silence.]
May these three impulses thrive within you,
assisting you in continuing to build a sense of
community one with another,
around this table,
and one with another out there in the wider county that
holds us all.
May the spirit of courage,
the spirit of compassion,
the spirit of commitment,

sustain you, your families, and your constituents,
through all that today and tomorrow will bring.
So may it be. *Shalom. Amen.*

—BETH GRAHAM
Suffolk County legislative meeting invocation

Meditation on Peace

LET US HOLD LOVINGLY IN OUR THOUGHTS all the people of the earth:
those who are consumed by mutual hatred and bitterness;
those who make bloody war upon their neighbors;
those who oppress their brothers and sisters
with any form of tyranny;
and all who suffer in subjection, cruelty, and injustice.
Let us recognize our solidarity with all the outcast,
with the downtrodden, the abused, the deprived,
and our common humanity with all who bear the
responsibilities of leadership and power.
Let us remember humanity's ancient and universal dream
of peace:
that we live together in harmony,
no one exploiting the weak, no one hating the strong,
each of us working out our own destiny,
self-respecting and unafraid.

May we seek to be worthy of freedom,
free from institutional wrong,
free from individual oppression and contempt,
pure of heart and hand,
despising none, defrauding none,
giving to all people in all encounters of life
the honor due to those who, like us,
are children of the earth's great love.

—KENDYL GIBBONS

Let Peace Flow

LET US JOIN IN A SPIRIT OF QUIET MEDITATION.

Let Peace flow into you. Let it calm your troubled self, heal your needy self, help your angry self to remember to listen—fully and compassionately—to the Other.

Let Peace flow around you, until you walk with peace and speak words of peace and reflect all the radiance of this beautiful world.

Let Peace flow through you and beyond you. Let peace guide you and fill you with wisdom. Let it be the bridge that connects you, not just with people of good will but also with people whose hearts are centered in their own needs and desires, who are not yet free to bring peace into their hearts.

Let Peace fill the world. Let it begin now. Here. Today.

We ask this in the name of that power that dwells within us and beyond us:

a power called by many names in many times and places, but whose universal name is *Love.*

—Eileen Karpeles

interfaith peace group dinner invocation

Where Shall I Seek Peace?

Shalom—how magical the sound.
Pacem—how lofty the thought.
Salaam—how welcome the feeling.
Peace—how far the journey.
The world seems at war with itself:
There are strident voices among people,
there are clashes among groups,
there are conflicts among nations.
The world seems to be nothing so much as a battleground,
strewn with the wreckage of people, hurt and afraid.
Be it within the walls of a house,
the confines of a city,
the boundaries of a nation,
or the broader reaches of the globe,

Peace is sought in vain.
Where shall I seek peace?
In the halls of men and women of state?
Where shall I seek peace?
In the chambers of politicians?
Where shall I seek peace?
In the bosom of the family?

—RICHARD GILBERT
Center for Peace meeting

Prepare Our Hearts to Be at Peace

WE GATHER ONCE AGAIN to do God's work, the work of peace.
May we seek to renew a right spirit within our own souls,
and a right spirit among our sisters and brothers gathered
    here today,
so that we might carry the Spirit of the God of Peace into
    the world,
to relieve the suffering of all sentient beings.
Reaching inward, we prepare our hearts to be at peace,
to work with our colleagues in peace, and to bring peace to
    the world.
We hear the words of our teachers,
echoing the understanding and wisdom of our many

spiritual traditions.

And so now, as we turn to our work at this meeting, mindful
of our cosmic companionship,

let us pray with our actions for peace in the nations, and in
the cities.

May this be a reflection of the peace that resides in each of
our hearts.

May our greatest passion be compassion and our greatest
strength be love.

So may it be. *Amen. Shalom. Salaam.*

—DENNIS M. DAVIDSON
Fellowship of Reconciliation National Council meeting

When There Is Peace in the Heart

IN THE HOLY CALM AND PEACE of this time and place, we
share the strength of the various faiths that sustain us.

May our common purpose as peacemakers cut across all
creeds and remind us of the mystic oneness
by which all peoples of the earth are bound together.

We are held together by an invisible link with the earth
on which we live and move
and have our being.

We are members, one of another, sharing humanity's joys

and sorrows, victories and defeats.
We are citizens of one humanity, nestled together to strive
for the common good.
We are actors on the stage of history,
bound to one another by a common destiny
of weal and woe.
We are sparks of divinity,
glowing in a cosmos whose origin and destiny
we do not know,
but whose mystery we celebrate.
As we partake of this common meal,
may we be mindful that throughout our world
there are millions who live daily with want and war—and
others who live with prosperity and peace—appetites
without dinners at one end of humanity's table,
and dinners without appetites at the other.
In the name of that which sustains us in our various faiths,
may we be thankful for the food we are about to receive.
May it be blessed to our use,
and may we be dedicated to the service of that great
family of all souls.
When there is peace in the heart,
there will be gentleness in the person.
When there is gentleness in the person,
there will be fairness in the nation.

When there is fairness in the nation,
  there will be peace in the world.
May we be centers of peace and help speed the day.
Amen.

—RICHARD GILBERT
Center of Peace invocation

We Pause to Give Thanks

WE PAUSE IN THE MIDST OF OUR BUSY DAY,
joining with others across our globe,
Who, like us, yearn for peace;
Who, like us, yearn for the day when
all men and women and children
can live together in harmony and understanding.
We pause here, in this special place,
to remember noble words and courageous acts
that have given us the peace we enjoy
and have urged us forward in the quest
for a more peaceful world.
We pause to celebrate the joy of people coming together,
serving one another with common goals and concerns,
helping the downtrodden,
sheltering the homeless,

feeding the hungry,
caring for the children.
We pause to ask God's blessing
on this our time together,
on gatherings like ours,
across our land and across the world.
We ask God's blessing
on the deliberations of the United Nations
as the General Assembly convenes this day.
May the leaders who gather to deliberate
the many issues that separate and divide us
be given eyes to see
and ears to hear
and the willingness to participate in the ways of peace.
We ask God's blessing
that the work of our hands will be fruitful,
the meditations of our hearts will bring love,
and the words of our mouths will bear wisdom
as we seek to walk in the paths of peace ourselves.
We give thanks for all that has sustained us in the past,
And look forward with hope
to the day our world will be one. *Amen.*

—LAUREL HALLMAN
United Nations peace celebration

Prayer for Justice in the Marketplace

IN THE CENTER OF THIS TEEMING city, with the sights and sounds of a working city surrounding us, we utter a prayer for justice in the marketplace. We meet here to give support to working people who strive to support their families, who seek some semblance of security in their lives.

We are mindful of the cries of the prophets of every time and tradition, who have spoken about justice pouring down like waters and righteousness like a mighty stream. We are mindful of those courageous souls in every age and clime who have spoken truth to power. We are mindful of one prophet who so identified with the poor that he said it was easier for a camel to go through the eye of a needle than for a rich man to enter the Kingdom of God.

In this center city space, we realize we are all neighbors — workers and management, rich and poor, city and suburb. We would seek, then, simply to be neighborly toward one another—treating our neighbors as ourselves, treating our neighbors as we would like to be treated—that justice might prevail.

The quest for justice is a lonely, hard road. We lift up our voices to pray for justice—that those of us who hunger might have bread, and that those of us who have bread might have the hunger for justice. *Amen.*

—RICHARD GILBERT

Prayer for Victims of Violence

IN THE MIDST OF THIS NOISY CITY, where violence is too much with us, in a land teeming with rancor, we lift up our prayer of life to the Holy, by whatsoever name we may call it.

We pray for the victims of violence, those whose loved ones have been taken from them, that they might be healed in their hurt and come to forgive. We pray, too, for the perpetrators of violence, that they might be redeemed and made whole, and learn to live in peace. And we pray for those who have been executed by the State, that their families might be made whole.

We pray for those of us who are torn and tormented by angry voices, vindictive voices, and for those who are tempted to join them. May we have the courage to reject vengeance, restore the wholeness of community, and bring reconciliation.

The road to peace and non-violence is a hard way; the temptations to vengeance are many; may we encourage the better angels of our nature and become messengers of peace and good will. May we be the peacemakers and the life-affirmers who are harbingers of Beloved Community. In the name of the Most Holy we pray. *Amen.*

— RICHARD GILBERT

HEALING AND REMEMBRANCE

Prayer for Desert Times

THE JOURNEYS OF OUR LIVES are never fully charted.
There come, sometimes, to each of us, deserts to cross,
barren stretches
    where the green edge on the horizon may be our
    destination,
    or an oasis on our way,
    or a mirage that beckons and will leave us lost.
When fear grips the heart, or despair bows the head,
    may we bend as heart and head lead us down
    to touch the ground beneath our feet,
and scoop some sand into our hands,
    and receive what the sand would teach us:

It holds the warmth of the sun when the sun has
    left our sight,
    as it holds the cool of the night when the stars have faded.
And hidden among its grains are tiny seeds, at rest and
    waiting.
Dormant, yet undefeated. Desert flowers.
They endure.
Moistened by our tears,
    and by the rain that comes to end even the longest
    drought,
    they send down roots, and they bloom.

Oh, may we believe in those seeds,
    and the seeds within us.
May we remember in our dry seasons
    that we, too, are desert flowers.
Amen.

—MARGARET KEIP

A Tiny Wellspring, a Thundering River

THE STORY IS TOLD OF A HIKER who enjoyed vacationing in the wooded ravines of northern Wisconsin. One day he came across a beautiful, crystal-clear rivulet of pure spring water. Warm from his hike, he improvised a drinking cup out of the crown of his hat and, after dipping it into the brook, he took a long, satisfying drink of sparkling water.

The hiker decided to follow the winding stream up the valley to its source. Hidden deep in the recesses of the forest, the water was bubbling up from a mossy bed and sparkled like the purest diamonds in the sunlight. Yet the font of the spring was so small that he could literally cover the spot of origin with the palm of his hand. Even so, he could not stop the flow. The water oozed through his fingers and made its way down the valley, singing gaily as it went about its journey of mercy—to carry its life-sustaining blessing to bird and beast, to flower and field—leaving everything in its path green and beautiful, healthier and happier.

This assembly, this day, has been set aside to honor the memory of a single, solitary, humble life. The life of a man who both *had* a dream and *lived* that dream. Like the tiny font of the river in our parable, the man we honor this day was a wellspring. His ideals, his convictions, his faith bubbled up from their sacred source within and pushed through the mossy overgrowth of bigotry and intolerance, bursting forth into the light of a better day. Though the point of origin may have been small, a mighty river of morality and social commitment has truly flowed forward from it. Though some tried to block the brook's flow—some tried, oh, so mightily—nevertheless, as the Psalmist declared: "The Eternal One projected truth forward—and nothing could stifle its inevitable surge ahead." (Psalm 57:53)

We gather together this day, on the banks of a truly majestic river of thought that has made its way out from its modest source and traveled on its journey of mercy until, eventually, it has touched every haven and hamlet across this great nation. It is none other than the river of liberty and justice for all, which offers its life-sustaining message to men and women of every race and creed—leaving everything in its path green and beautiful, healthier and happier.

And so, dear friends, let us pause to give thanks to the Source of All Life for having placed this courageous dreamer in our midst.

We ought truly to be grateful for the manifold blessings that have come to us as a birthright—even as we rededicate ourselves, on this day in particular, to the thundering admonition of the prophet: "Do justly, love mercy, and walk humbly with your God." *(Micah 6:8)*

Thankful are we for those unrelenting visionaries—for men and women whose towering faith constitutes a veritable wellspring of hope that nourishes our spiritual hungers and fortifies our wavering souls.

May the words of our mouths, and the meditations of our hearts, be acceptable before you, O Source of All Life, our strength and support.

—GARY P. ZOLA
Martin Luther King Day commemorative program invocation

Singing a New Song

THERE COMES A TIME—to break the silence.
There comes a time—to move beyond the fear.
There comes a time—to speak one's truth, even if it will not
    be welcome.
There comes a time—to call into question what has gone
    before;
    to resist the weight of the past.
There comes a time—for the singing of a new song,
    for a different way of being,
    for the claiming of power.
There comes a time—when the truth shall at last make us
    free.

One day, blessedly, the practiced lie dies on our lips,
    and the truth becomes more precious than the same,
    and the pretending ends.
There comes a time—when somehow courage finds us,
    or we find courage,
    and we dare to know who we are, and what we love.
There comes a time—when friends are there,
    holding us so gently in their love
    that all at once the impossible is possible,
    and we cross over to the other side
    of whatever bondage held us.
There comes a time—when the truth at last makes us free,
    and in that moment is the salvation of the world.

— KENDYL GIBBONS
National Coming Out Day

For Those Who Are Wounded or Fearful

O HOLY ONE, SOURCE of Strength and Infinite Compassion,
we turn to You now in a spirit of hope and openness.
Upon the gentle altar of Your care for us,
we place, as best we are able,
our sorrows and our regrets;
our longing and our woundedness;
the worries that circle round and round within us,
leaving our minds unable to rest.
If there be any among us now who feel overcome with fear,
we pray that they receive the comfort of renewed courage.
If there be any among us now who feel lost in loneliness,
we pray that they receive the tender healing that comes
    from connection to others.
If there be any among us now who feel imprisoned,
    shackled either outwardly or inwardly,
we pray from our hearts for their liberation,
that they might be—each in their own way—set free once again.
Let us know that You are with us.
Let us trust that You are for us.
Let us experience the mysterious and sacred power of Your
    movement among us. *Amen.*

—GRETCHEN THOMPSON
prayer for the patients on a locked mental health unit

Prophet in the Wilderness of Racism

AND IT CAME TO PASS in those days that the spirit of God
visited a young woman whose name was Rosa.
God multiplied her strength and her determination. She
would not be moved.
And all Montgomery looked upon her and wondered.
And God raised up a prophet in the midst of that people,
whose name was Martin, that the courage of Rosa
should not perish, but that it should be extended and
multiplied, and indeed it was done.
For the words of the prophet fell upon the ears of the nation.
The people listened. A dream was dreamed, a vision was
provided, a highway was created through the desert of
racism.
The lowly and the ignored were lifted up and exalted, and in
the rough places—Selma, Atlanta, Birmingham, Memphis,
Boston, Washington, D.C.—the truth was made plain.

But the plain truth was denied. The prophet was slain. Thick
darkness covered the land.
Yet the promise declared by the prophet would not be
overcome.
In the darkness the light continues to shine; the people are
called forth, their strength doubled, their vision

extended, for the spirit of God is upon them, and the time is at hand that they should deliver the nation from cynicism and despair.

And so it is given to us in these latter days that by our efforts (as God shall help us) the oppressed shall receive justice, the righteous shall receive their reward, and peace shall flow down like a mighty stream, as the prophet Martin did declare it unto us.
Let the people assembled say, *Amen.*

—VICTOR CARPENTER
Martin Luther King, Jr. breakfast

Honoring Those Who Died

WE COME TOGETHER TO SEEK meanings beyond our limited selves. We come together to seek a spirit that binds together the scattered threads of our humanity; a thread that binds us together in sympathy, in understanding, in love; a thread that weaves the past, present, and future together and unites the fragments of our existence into a meaningful whole.

Since we have felt the sense of death, since we have borne its dread, life has grown more dear. Since we have felt the sense of death, the gift of life is more a jewel, and the thread that binds us together is much more precious.

And, since we have gathered to honor the memories of departed friends, loved ones, and co-workers, and to recognize through awards the ongoing thread of life that carries us into the future, let our hearts and minds and spirits be filled with gratitude for all those who give deep meaning to our lives. In the spirit of love and joy, may God's presence grace us this day.

—SUSAN SUCHOCKI BROWN
Firefighters Memorial Sunday

Prayer on the Violent Death of a Child

OUR HEARTS CRY OUT, "Please no, please make it not be so.
It cannot be, that any kind of Holiness
would suffer this,
the violent loss among us of a beautiful child, an innocent,
one so vulnerable and open-hearted to the world."
We gather together now in a grieving all but unbearable,
a grieving riddled with anger, distrust, guilt, and regret.
We would beg You now for consolation,
but can only speak the one lonely word: Why?

Help us to fathom the unfathomable;
to offer comfort to others out of our own deep
  woundedness;
to release our bitterness in ways that will not continue the
  violence;
to recognize and embrace kindness in the midst of cruelty;
to find hope in the midst of overwhelming doubt,
And Life, somehow, in the dark and bloody midst of this
  Death, which consumes us.
We would serve Love, but need help finding our way. *Amen.*

—GRETCHEN THOMPSON

Give Us, O God

GIVE US, O GOD, O LIFE, O MIND,
  sense to see beyond the timidities of time and the
  failures of vision.
Help us to help ourselves to cross the cold creek of
  callousness
  and to skirt the tangled briers of easy doubt.
Help us to help each other to avoid the chasms of cynicism
  as well as the crippling comforts of complacency.
May we believe, but not easily;
  doubt, but not quickly;

disbelieve, but with good reason,
and be dedicated only to the best of knowledge.
Help us to walk the narrow path between blind faith and
bitter disillusionment.

— MAX COOTS

GRATITUDE AND PRAISE

Remembering Those Who Make
Our Lives More Holy

As we gather here this morning—many of us with sleep still heavy on our eyes—let us pause for a moment to remember the faces of those who have shaped our lives:

the mentor who gave us unstintingly from his or her vast store of experience and wisdom;

the colleague who allowed us to acknowledge our imperfections by telling us of her own;

the son or daughter whose quiet wisdom and good humor made us ashamed of our own pettiness;

the enemy who fought us fairly—and forgave us when
we won;

the beloved Other whose touch has made us whole,
not once, but again and again.

Our days and nights are rescued from the void of
meaninglessness—our lives are made holy—by the unearned
generosity of the countless ordinary human beings who travel
the road with us. Let us respond by passing on to others the
joy and the grave courtesy and the kindliness with which they
have graced our lives, teaching us (through their actions) what
it means to be religious persons.

We ask this in the name of all that we, in our separate
traditions, deem holy and sustaining: the great unknowable
power that keeps us on the pathway of love.

—EILEEN KARPELES
chamber of commerce breakfast invocation

On Women Who Dream

SPIRIT OF LIFE, IN WHOSE IMAGE we are both male and female, we pause on this special occasion to give thanks—for we have been given many blessings, and we have come very far. In this Women's Equality Week, we think especially of our mothers and grandmothers, and their mothers and grandmothers, whose yearning stretched forward into this our time, in their best hopes for us. Women who stitched, and cooked, and cleaned, who chastised and challenged their sons and daughters alike—sowing the seeds of equality at the hearthside of their homes. Women who dreamed of a future when life would be easier, the gifts of life more fully available to all who live, and who taught their children that it could be so. For all our foremothers, O God, who brought us to this celebration, we are grateful.

We give thanks for the women who donned their white dresses and green ribbons and gathered themselves together to give voice to their yearnings—for the vote, for the freedom to participate in a larger life and accept responsibility for the course of human destiny, alongside men. We remember their courage in the face of hostility, their dignity in the face of humiliation, and their tenacity in the face of discouragement. For all their gifts to us, we are grateful.

We give thanks, O God, for the men who listened to the women's hopes, who shared power, who honored Your larger truth, and who enlarged their lives in the process. For we all have been blessed.

O Thou who continues to call us to be better than we are, our prayer is that we might carry forward the gifts of equality with honor and courage, now and in the days to come, for there is much, much more to be done. Bless now the deliberations of this day, and the men and women of this council as they guide our city forward, into the future. This is our prayer. *Amen.*

—LAUREL HALLMAN
city council invocation during Women's Equality Week

Eternal Spirit, We Thank You

DEAR ETERNAL SPIRIT
    who gives us Life, Breath, and Love:
    we thank You for these gifts.
Help us to be ever-mindful of these gifts,
    to bear them in joy and responsibility.
Help us to enter into this life we have been given,
    to enter into each moment as a rare treasure,

to listen for the silent music
in the spheres, and
in each other.
Help us to accept love as it comes to us,
to see clearly the invisible boundaries,
to rest in the Universal Love of all Creation,
as a small boat can rest
in a placid, endless sea.
So we rest in Thee, Eternal Spirit.
Help us to say "Yes" to life,
to answer, "Here Am I,"
to live and breathe words and songs
of this Love we know is shared,
or can be:
Love given and received,
in every breath,
in every word,
in every song,
every day.
Dear Eternal Sprit,
who gives us Life, Breath, and Love:
we thank You for these gifts.

— PEGGY S. BLOCK
interfaith meeting

Prayer for a Community in Transition

LOVING GOD, THANK YOU for the gift of family and
   community,
   for the life and love we share.
We ask you to make us aware of your presence
   during this time of transition.
Help us to know that we are not alone
   in life's comings and goings.
Help us to accept change as an opportunity to grow
   in our trust and understanding of each other and you.
Help us to refocus on who we are
   and what we are about.
Remind us that change can bring new energy,
   new life, and a re-commitment to all we hold sacred.
Grant us the security of knowing we rest
   in the faithfulness of your care.
May this period of transition be a time of transformation,
   allowing us to become all we are to be.

— JUDITH DUNLAP

Gratitude for What We May Take for Granted

SPIRIT OF ALL GIFTS AND GRACE,

We are not ungrateful—not all the time.

We know that life is a precious gift. Though we would
appear at times to squander it, remember the ways we
do not:

When we are happy, accept our joy as gratitude for all
opportunities, accepted and ignored.

When we are broken, accept our tears and anger as gratitude
for feeling deeply.

When we reach out to others, accept our compassion as
gratitude for conscience and compassion.

When we choose solitude, accept our silence as gratitude for
the deepness of spirit we are seeking.

When we act thoughtlessly, accept our mistakes as gratitude
for the freedom we have in our lives.

When we act foolishly, accept our lapses as gratitude for the
lessons we have yet to learn.

When we share our stories, accept the telling of our lives as
gratitude for community and family.

When we worship, accept our ritual mumblings as symbols
of gratitude for all they represent.

Spirit of Thanksgiving, when we remember to give thanks for
life and love, for knowledge and wisdom, for freedom to

act and for freedom from oppression, accept our
obvious omissions as unspoken gratitude for suffering
that brings us compassion, for sorrow that helps us
grow, for disappointment that gives us determination, for
illness that offers healing, and for death that makes way
for new cycles of life and creation.
Amen.

—L. ANNIE FOERSTER
Thanksgiving Eve prayer service

Let Us Be Grateful

LET US GIVE THANKS,
for we are blessed with heads that we may think clearly.
We give thanks.
Let us be grateful,
for we are blessed with hearts of loyalty.
We are grateful.
Let us give thanks,
for we are blessed with hands with the potential for great
    service.
We give thanks.
Let us be grateful,

for we are blessed with health that leads to better living.
We are grateful.
May we bestow such blessing on our club, our community,
and our country. *Amen.*

—KATIE STEIN SATHER
grace for a 4-H dinner

Prayer of Petition
(When You Don't Know What You Want or Need)

SPIRIT OF AGES, LIGHT OF LIFE,
What can we tell that is not already known?
What can we ask for that will not come without the asking?
And, still we speak—to tell, to ask, to pray.
We would tell of our triumphs, in order to drown out the
shout of our defeats;
we would tell of our love, in order to still the fear that we
are unloved;
and we would tell of our lives, as if to live forever.
We would ask for wisdom, and will settle for the courage to
do what we must;
We would ask for joy, and will be grateful for the ability
to cry;

And we would ask for one another's continued presence,
and will be content with memories and dreams.
Thus we tell; and thus we ask; and thus we pray:
Giving thanks for what has been, accepting what is, and
yearning with hope and determination for what will be.
Amen.

—L. ANNIE FOERSTER

Gratitude for Your Bounty

SOURCE OF ALL THAT IS, was, will be, Loving Spirit moving
in and through all,
We call ourselves to awareness of your presence.
In awe and wonder,
we remember your power and grace,
the beauty of the world you have given us,
the amazing diversity of life,
the richness of the challenges of creation to which you call us.
You remind us to care for and about one another and all
creation,
to be worthy stewards, responsible for our part in process.
We are grateful for the gifts and the challenges.
We are grateful for brothers and sisters

who rise to the call to give generously and fully of time,
	energy, and money.
As we gather today,
may we never forget your bounty and our gratitude,
nor discount the challenges to which you continue to call us.
We are indeed blessed by generosity.
May we always honor and fulfill our promises with love to
	you.
So be it! Blessed be! Shalom! Amen!

—GRETCHEN WOODS
United Way luncheon

What Can Save Us?

WE ARE TEMPTED TO DESPAIR.
The world is prone to mayhem and disaster.
Why bother? Who cares? What's the use?
What can save us from this temptation to despair? A deeply
	held attitude of thankfulness.
From thankfulness arises hope; from hope, joy; from joy,
	wonder.
"In everything, give thanks," wrote St. Paul.
Thankfulness will be our strength in times of weakness.

Thankfulness will be our lamp in times of darkness.
Thankfulness will be our companion in times of loneliness.
Go in gratitude for the gifts of Life and Love.
Go in appreciation for the presence of one another.
Go as thankful people to tempt the world to joy.
Blessed be. Amen.

—L. ANNIE FOERSTER
Thanksgiving Day

Creation in Three-Quarter Time with Mixed Metaphor

THERE WAS SPACE, BUT NO BEGINNING,
and in the space were spaces,
and between the spaces, stars.
They moved about—space, and spaces, and stars—
a kind of celestial progressive dinner without food,
a kind of heavenly musical chairs without a loser.

And their movements made Music—swish, and bang, and hum;
and their music made Dancing—sway, and step, and bow;
and their dancing made Intimacy—come, and stay, and join;
and their Intimacy made Possibility and Potential—Hmmm,
and Maybe, and Yes!

A kind of blind date between old friends;
a kind of dream without sleeping.

Possibility was Egg; Potential was Seed.
And the Possible Egg hatched, and spawned, and bore.
And the Potential Seed sowed, and sprouted, and bloomed.
And Egg and Seed combined and made Creation.
a kind of Mardi Gras in July without Lent;
a kind of memorial service for Silence and Emptiness
without Regret.

There was creation in space.
There was creativity in the spaces.
The stars blazed with creatures and creators.
And everywhere there was—and is—Music:
Listen within you;
And everywhere there was—and is—Dancing:
Look around you;
And Possibility and Potential are ever again Intimate:
Look between us.

And the eggs are within the male, and the female,
and the other—everything is Possibility.
And the seeds are within the female, and the male,
and the other—everything is Potential.

And the music is Dance, and the Dancing is Intimacy, and the
Intimacy is Song.
A kind of cosmic choir in tap shoes without program or score.

—L. ANNIE FOERSTER

The Hollow of His Hands, The Curve of Her Arms

LET US PRAY TO THE GOD WHO HOLDS US in the hollow of
    his hands,
to the God who holds us in the curve of her arms,
to the God whose flesh is the flesh of hills and
    hummingbirds and angleworms,
whose skin is the color of an old black woman and a young
    white man,
    and the color of the leopard and the grizzly bear and the
    green grass snake,
whose hair is like the aurora borealis, rainbows, nebulae,
    waterfalls, and a spider's web,
whose eyes sometimes shine like the evening star,
    and then like fireflies, and then again like an open wound,
whose touch is both the touch of life and the touch of
    death,
and whose name is everyone's, but mostly mine.

And what shall we pray?
Let us say, "Thank you."
Amen.

—MAX COOTS

Earth Prayer

MOTHER EARTH, WE ARE GATHERED HERE this morning to bask in your beauty and reflect on your place in our lives. Too often we forget how you feed us, whisper in our ears, and sprinkle our sleep with dreams. Help us to remember that through you we are all joyfully connected.

We pray for your presence among us, Great Mother. Our burdens can be great, and we feel alone. Our hands have not felt the touch of another, and our hearts long for reconciliation, compassion, and understanding.

Now, on this day, we open our hearts to you and to one another. We breathe in your love, and feel that we are worthy of love. We feel your touch, and know that we are touched. We pray for the well-being of all creatures on the earth, for your spirit, Mother Earth, lives within, and connects us all. Thank you for the many gifts and blessing in our lives. As we give love, may we also receive love. *Amen.*

—SHARON DITTMAR

DEDICATIONS AND ORDINATIONS

To Build a Bridge

Who has measured the waters in the hollow of his hand and marked
off the heavens with a span? Isaiah 40:12 (NRSV)

O GOD, CREATIVE ONE, SUSTAINER OF LIFE, Eternal Spirit
of Love, hear our prayers!
We lift up our hearts to you, Creator of Life,
who laid the foundations of the earth,
and determined the measurements of the universe,
who has held the waters of the earth in the hollow of
your hand, and stretched the span of the heavens across
all time and space.

We give thanks today for the abundant gifts of the earth and
of the sea, for the gifts of your creation which sustain us
continually and inspire the best of our own creative
endeavors.

We give thanks this morning,
for those whose long labors through many seasons
made this day of celebration possible:
for architects and ironworkers,
for electricians and engineers,
for leaders of cities and builders of roads.

We give thanks today for the gift of community:
for the human spirit and for Hope, Faith, and Love,
by which we bridge the tides of time.

For we know that we who celebrate today arrived at this
moment on the long ebb tide of history.

We are connected to the dreamers and the builders who
lived here and loved this place before us.

And we know that as we stand on this bridge today, the
future is flowing toward us.

We are connected also to the generations to come, who will
cross over and sail under this bridge
long after we are gone.

All of these citizens, too, are part of our community. We pray
that the remembrance of them will guide us always
toward the common good.

We stand today on a new gateway to the sea, to the waters of the bay that connects us to the great circle of the world ocean. We pray today for the wisdom to be good bridge-keepers, responsible stewards of the environment, always aware of the ways that human endeavors are linked to the great, interdependent web of all life you have created.

As we celebrate today the completion of this graceful ribbon of iron and granite, concrete and steel, we also pray for the vision and the perseverance necessary to build new bridges of opportunity, justice, and equality within our communities. We who are connected by the bridge are African-American, European-American, Asian-American, and Native American. We are women and men, girls and boys, young and old, gay and straight. We come to you through many ancient traditions of faith, or none at all. We arrived here long ago, or just yesterday. May all of us aspire to become a community that is always building new bridges.

On this joyous day, we offer our prayers to you, Eternal Creator, in the name of all we hold most sacred. Amen and Blessed Be!

— JILL JOB SAXBY
opening of a new bridge

Why Bouquets Have Nettles

SPIRITS OF LOVE AND CREATION, which dwell in our midst today: Grant three blessings to the members of this community for their abiding prosperity.

May their far-sighted vision of possibilities inherent in this great venture be dimmed to expedient myopia, so they may not be frightened by the arduousness of the path just ahead.

May their warm joy of fellowship in one another's company be occasionally chilled by winds of controversy and icicles of contention, to remind them that the greenhouse of community is fine for starting seeds, but that deep roots and strong branches are encouraged by a diversity of elements, some of them harsh.

And, in the blossoming bouquets and laurels of their success, sweet smelling with victory and bright colored with jubilation, may they find an uncommon nettle to sting them into new achievements, and the threads of a spinning spider to remind them of the interdependent web of all things, all communities, and all people, of which they are a very important and welcome part. *Amen.*

—L. ANNIE FOERSTER
dedication of a new church

For Those Who Died So Our Country Might Live

THIS DAY, BY ALL THE POWER GIVEN US, let us dedicate this cemetery's memorial to those who have died in service to our country, to the sacred hope for peace.

We have constructed a memorial to those who have served our country and sacrificed their lives. Woe to us if we cannot give them honor in this moment! We are here this afternoon to dedicate these stones to the hopes that were cut short. Thus, from all we owe, we fashion a symbol from which a new hope may grow.

May the living who owe so much come to encounter the dead who have sacrificed so greatly. Every name written on this stone is precious beyond what we can reckon. Their names are their eternities. What honor we are able to give them, now and in future time, will be the substance of our hope.

Let us pray that we will remember them. We recount their names. We recognize their lives were just like ours—with loves, with strengths and weaknesses, with limitations and shining moments of courage, with struggles and agonies, with bursts of anger and bursts of laughter, with dawn and dusk, with joys and sorrows—with all the things so necessary to real living. They were us and we are them here in this place. There is nothing here anymore that can serve to separate the living and dead.

May the silence here speak to us: the silence of mothers and fathers fighting fiercely against a pain that can never be eased, the silence of lovers, spouses and children in inconsolable grief, the silence of a world searching inward for the meaning of war and the possibility of peace, the silence of souls seeking to know but one more thing: the ultimate purpose of their deaths.

— MARK ALLSTROM
dedication of veterans' memorial

May Their Need Be Answered

WE COME IN THE SPIRIT OF LOVE and caring. We come here to open our spirits to the Great Spirit. We come here to open our souls to the Oversoul. We come here to dedicate this chapel to all that is holy and to give thanks to our God.

People in need will use this place to utter heart-felt prayers, seeking, praising and thanking God with the name their own traditions have given. Their prayers, their needs, will be heard. So we, humbly, gather this day to honor this house of worship for all faiths and to dedicate it by simply praying that the prayers of those who will use this place in future time will reach high. May their need be answered.

— MARK ALLSTROM
rededication of hospital's interfaith chapel

Written on the Heart

I BEGIN WITH A PARABLE. When he was a boy, Joseph Levy carved his name on a tree in his backyard and thought to himself: "Now, everybody who passes by this tree will remember the name Joseph Levy." At the same time, he chiseled his name into a rock that was perched high on the top of a cliff near his home. He thought to himself: "Now, everybody who passes by this boulder will remember the name Joseph Levy."

Years later, as an adult, Joseph returned to his childhood home and looked for the tree he had not seen in many years. He discovered that the tree had been felled by a logger's ax long ago. His name, carved into its trunk, had vanished with the tree.

As with the tree, he discovered that the boulder had been quarried. The once mighty rock had been hammered into pebbles. His name, once chiseled into its veneer, had vanished with the rock.

In time Joseph Levy became successful. With his wealth, he decided to erect an imposing structure. This new building, he determined, would be called "The Joseph Levy Building." He thought to himself: "Now, everybody who passes by this grand edifice will remember the name Joseph Levy."

But years later, a fire burned the building, name and all, to the ground. Discouraged, and despairing of ever making his name great, Joseph resolved to share his remaining wealth with worthy causes and people in need. One day he went to the ward of a hospital and distributed toys to the children who were ill. One little girl looked up with gratitude in her eyes and said: "Thank you, Mr. Levy. I will never forget you."

He smiled and answered: "Thank *you*. That was a very sweet thing to say, but I am afraid that in time, you will indeed forget."

"Oh, no," the child responded. "I will *never* forget you. You see, your name is written on my heart."

We have gathered together today to dedicate this new hospital structure. We know that, over time, human suffering will be eased in the corridors of this building. Devastating illnesses will be cured within its halls. Yet at a time such as this, we would be wise to remember that the true distinction of this building will never be found in the words written on its facade, or in the bricks and mortar of which it is composed. This new hospital facility will become a center of healing only because the people who labor inside each and every day strive to write their names on the hearts of their fellow beings, whom they have chosen to serve.

Thankful are we for the many blessings this great house of healing, its staff and benefactors, have given to our community for so many years.

We are grateful for the strength we find in the company of those dedicated to healing the body and the mind, to acts of loving-kindness, and to the betterment of the human condition.

In this spirit of dedication, we rely on the words of the Psalmist of old in expressing our deeply felt sentiments of thanksgiving—both for what we have already achieved, and for what we may yet be permitted to accomplish: "Let the favor of the Eternal One be upon us; let all that we put our hands to prosper. O prosper the work of our hands!" *(Psalm 91:17)*

—GARY P. ZOLA
dedication of a hospital

May Love Hallow Every Home

AND NOW MAY LOVE HALLOW EVERY HOME
    that has been built on this magnificent space;
may Peace anoint every heart that shall dwell here;
may the light of Kindness bless new friendships that shall
    form on these streets;
may Joy find its way into this new neighborhood of
    childhood dreams and delights;
and may Hope make these houses into homes and places of
    haven from all the vicissitudes of life.

—GARY E. SMITH
benediction of a new affordable housing site

A Home for Rest, Peace, and Love

Lord,

Take care for this place.
Here lie the elemental traces of those who loved
    this home of warmth, acceptance, and support.
Here is a place where is enshrined the quest
    of those who love God;
    those who celebrated human strivings for love,
    peace, and justice;
    those who found in earth and nature an answer;
    those whose quest had not yet found answers.
Find in this place rest, peace, and love.

— Jim Berry
dedication of memorial garden

To Serve the Good of All

Dear Holy and infinite Source of love, mercy, justice, and righteousness, your prophet Amos looked around at his world and pronounced to all, "Let Justice roll down like waters and righteousness like an ever-flowing stream," and today we have gathered in this hallowed place to be reminded of the ancient and sacred duty to which we dedicate ourselves today—that is, to establish and to uphold society with justice. Holy and special is the purpose for which we have gathered, and we have been granted a unique opportunity today. We have been granted the gift of time and a cease from the usual hustle and bustle of the day to reflect on the grand purpose for which this courthouse is so dedicated.

May these walls, strengthened and cleansed, remind us that we too must have our souls, our bodies, our hearts in good order when we enter here to speak words of justice and mercy.

May this space now dedicated remind us that we are called to dedicate our lives to a higher purpose than just ourselves.

May that source that we serve, be it called God, or law, or humanity, or love, enter with you who walk through these doors each day, and may it ease the suffering of all.

May we know that the words we speak, the truths we seek, the judgments we render, the punishments, the rehabilitations proposed here, are meant to serve the good of all humanity.

May we know that when all the people of the world love, that when justice is tempered with mercy, that when righteousness and virtue walk arm in arm, we will be doing the best that we can for the good of our lives, careers, and duties.

I ask, Dear God, that this place be blessed and the people who serve here be blessed and protected. *Amen.*

—SUSAN SUCHOCKI BROWN
dedication of courthouse

Prayer for the Blessing and Dedication of Animals

MY FURRY, FEATHERED, AND SCALED friends, I greet you. You come from the same life force of creation that I do and I greet you as a sister.

I pray that your days be filled with love and whatever else you desire. May your tummy always be full and may you always have a place to rest. I pray you have many days of love with your human friends. May you play together and work together in gentleness and respect for one another.

Will participants please repeat after me: "I offer you this food as a token of my love for you. May our relationship provide blessings for us both."

My furry, feathered, and scaled friends, I say farewell. I am happy to have met you. May your life be blessed.

—L. ANNIE FOERSTER

We All Speak

THE ORDINATION OF A NEW MINISTER is the right and responsibility of the ordaining congregation. But our history goes into the making of each new minister and our future depends upon what they do. Likewise, we uphold the priesthood of all believers and the interdependence of all creation. For these traditions, I ask that you stand and join hands so that no one in this hall is separate from the community of celebration. And I ask that those closest to the dais come forward to join the celebrant to this body. Through this chain of humanity, we bring our combined energies to this prayer of ordination. At the end of the prayer, I will ask for your shared voices saying the words I invite you to speak. Let us pray:

Ancient of Days, Impender of Destiny, we ask a blessing on our sister Virginia Sparling, as she embarks on her new venture and calling. May the past inspire her and the future beckon her on her journeys and her quests.

May she know in her darkest nights that the light of understanding awaits her if she seeks it truly. May she know in her greatest triumphs that this community celebrates with her. When she is lonely, let her remember our touch. When she is fulfilled, let her share that blessing with others.

May she in all moments of her ministry carry the knowledge of our presence, our affection, our concern, and our warmth, that she may know companionship even in solitude; that she may feel love even though all around her turn from her; that she may give solace to others out of her strength melded with ours; and that she always act with the heat of passion.

In this we all speak, saying "Amen." *Amen.*

In this we all speak, saying "Blessed Be." *Blessed Be.*

—L. ANNIE FOERSTER
ordination

This Sacred Moment

THIS IS A MOMENT OUTSIDE OF TIME. Grasp it and, with your presence, make it holy.

This is a dwelling outside of space. Inhabit it and, with your presence, make it sacred.

This is no ordinary thing we are called to do this evening. And we are no ordinary people who do it. If you invest in this moment, you can lend it the spirit of your hopes and dreams, grant it the soul of your vision and desire, give it the empowerment of your wisdom and love.

I call you to the ordination of one among us. I call you to the celebration of his commitment, his caring, and his concern. I call you, not to exalt him, but to accept him; not to worship him, but to cherish him; not to glorify him, but to welcome him; and not to set him apart, but to sustain him.

In this holy time, in this sacred space, I call you to do what only you can do: to enter fully and unreservedly into this covenant of ordination, and into this partnership of ministry.

Blessed be this sacred moment.

—L. ANNIE FOERSTER
ordination

Come We Now All Together

COME WE NOW OUT OF THE DARKNESS of unknowing, out of the dusk of dreaming.
Come we now from far places, from the unsolved mysteries of our beginnings.
Attend to the Journey!
Come we now into the twilight of awakening, into the reflection of our gathering.
Come we now toward the light that beckons, toward the oasis that summons.
Harken the gathering! Come we now all together.
We bring, unilluminated, our dark caves of doubting, filled with the rocks of our foreboding.

We seek, unbedazzled, the clear light of understanding, born
of the fires of our attending.
May the sparks of our joining
kindle our resolve,
brighten our spirits,
reflect our love,
and unshadow our days.
Come we now. Come we together. Come we now all
together to begin.
Let us begin with "Amen." *Amen.*

—L. ANNIE FOERSTER
ordination

ABOUT THE CONTRIBUTORS

MARK ALLSTROM has served churches in New York, South Carolina, and Massachusetts. He is currently minister of the Unitarian Church of South Australia, Adelaide, and president of Australia New Zealand Unitarians.

ELIZABETH O'SHAUGHNESSY BANKS serves as minister to the Unitarian Church of Davis, California.

VERN BARNETT has served since 1985 as minister in residence at the World Faiths Center for Religious Experience in Kansas City, Missouri.

JIM BERRY was a founding father and long-time member of Northern Hills Unitarian Universalist Fellowship in Cincinnati, Ohio, before his death in 2001.

PEGGY S. BLOCK is an oncology chaplain at Bridgeport Hospital in Bridgeport, Connecticut.

SUSAN SUCHOCKI BROWN is the parish minister at First Church Unitarian Universalist in Leominster, Massachusetts, as well as chaplain to the Leominster Fire Department.

JOHN BUEHRENS retired as president of the Unitarian Universalist Association in 2002, after serving the denomination for eight years in that capacity. He has returned to parish ministry at the First Parish in Needham, Massachusetts.

BURTON CARLEY has served as minister to First Unitarian Church of Memphis, Tennessee, since 1983.

VICTOR CARPENTER retired as senior minister of First Unitarian Church in Belmont, Massachusetts, in 2002.

MAX COOTS was named minister emeritus of the First Unitarian Church in Canton, New York, where he has served since 1958. He is author of *Seasons of the Self.*

GRETA CROSBY retired in 1996. She is minister emerita of both First Unitarian Universalist Church of Wichita, Kansas, and Unitarian Universalist Church of Yakima, Washington. Her book, *Tree and Jubilee*, was the 1983 Unitarian Universalist Association Meditation Manual.

CALVIN DAME is the minister of Unitarian Universalist Community Church in Augusta, Maine.

DENNIS M. DAVIDSON is a Unitarian Universalist community minister in Indian Wells, California.

SHARON DITTMAR is minister at First Unitarian Church in Cincinnati, Ohio.

JUDITH DUNLAP is a Roman Catholic lay woman who writes for St. Anthony Messenger Press in Cincinnati, Ohio.

L. ANNIE FOERSTER retired as minister of St. John's Unitarian Church in Cincinnati, Ohio, in 2001. She was named minister emerita of Evergreen Unitarian Church in Marysville, Washington, as well as minister emerita of St. John's.

KENDYL GIBBONS is minister at First Unitarian Society of Minneapolis, Minnesota. She has served on the Board of Trustees for Meadville/Lombard Theological School, and currently serves as president of the Unitarian Universalist Ministers Association.

RICHARD GILBERT is minister emeritus of First Unitarian Church at Rochester, New York. Among his published writings are the Unitarian adult curricula, *Building Your Own Theology*, and the 1995 Unitarian Universalist Association meditation manual, *In the Holy Quiet of This Hour.*

BETH GRAHAM serves as minister to the Unitarian Universalist Fellowship of Huntington, New York.

LAUREL HALLMAN is the senior minister of First Unitarian Church of Dallas, Texas.

JONALU JOHNSTONE serves as program minister to First Unitarian Church of Oklahoma City, and consulting minister at Channing Unitarian Universalist Church in Edmond, Oklahoma.

EILEEN KARPELES is a retired Unitarian Universalist accredited interim minister.

MARGARET KEIP is a Unitarian Universalist accredited interim minister after having served for twenty years as co-minister of the Unitarian Universalist Church of the Monterey Peninsula in Carmel, California, with her husband Fred. They were named minister emeriti of that congregation in 1996.

SUSAN MANKER-SEALE is minister of the Unitarian Universalist Congregation of Northwest Tucson, Arizona. She has served as president of Ministerial Sisterhood Unitarian Universalist (an organization of Unitarian Universalist clergy women).

KATHLEEN MCTIGUE is senior minister to the Unitarian Society of New Haven, Connecticut.

NORM NAYLOR is minister at Emerson Unitarian Universalist Church in Troy, Michigan.

PRISCILLA RICHTER is minister to First Unitarian Universalist Church of Indiana, Pennsylvania.

GEORGE A. ROBINSON III died in 2002 while serving as minister of the Unitarian Universalist Church of Flushing, New York.

Katie Stein Sather is taking a sabbatical year at her cabin in Newfoundland.

JILL JOB SAXBY is the newly called associate minister of The First Congregation Church, Unitarian Universalist in South Portland, Maine.

ROBERT SENGHAS is minister emeritus of First Unitarian Universalist Society in Burlington, Vermont.

GARY E. SMITH is senior minister at First Parish in Concord, Massachusetts. He served as president of the Unitarian Universalist Ministers Association from 1998 to 2001.

GRETCHEN THOMPSON is hospice chaplain for Health Partners in Minneapolis, Minnesota.

SUSAN M. WOLINSKY is a lay member of Northern Hills Unitarian Universalist Fellowship in Cincinnati, Ohio.

GRETCHEN WOODS is minister at the Unitarian Universalist Fellowship of Corvalis, Oregon. She has served as president of Ministerial Sisterhood Unitarian Universalist (an organization of Unitarian Universalist clergy women).

GARY P. ZOLA is a rabbi serving as director of the library at Hebrew Union College in Cincinnati, Ohio.

INDEX